I0008381

DATA STRUCTURE

In detail and comprehensively with the use of
programming examples in Python

First Edition

Eng. Khalil Jaber

Contents Part One:

Contents Part Two:

Introduction

Introduction:

This book seeks to be a comprehensive guide to understanding data structures and their applications. From basic concepts such as linked arrays and lists, to trees and hash tables, to advanced structures used in modern applications. It also aims to provide practical examples and practical exercises that help students and developers consolidate concepts and turn them into practical skills.

This book came to contribute to the enrichment of the library and to help the reader to understand the methods of data structures in depth, especially since it is the first book that deals with data structures in detail and comprehensively with the use of software examples in the Python language. The content of this book has been developed according to a course plan taught in many international universities and colleges.

Dear reader, please do not skimp on us with your comments and suggestions about this book, which I expect from you at the following address:

Khaliljaber99@gmail.com

Author
Khalil jaber

1. Basic concepts in data structures.
1.1 Data definition.

Data is a set of facts and ideas that have not been processed, and are considered the raw material for information. They are of limited utilization because they are not processed in the computer, are multi-sourced and are large.

1.2 Definition of Information.

Information is the results that we obtain after the data processing process, or it is the data after processing, and the benefit is more than the data, and it is limited sources and its size is less than the data. The following graphic shows us how information is obtained from data.

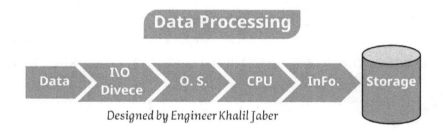

Figure (1) shows how to obtain information from data.

The following table shows the difference between data and information.

Teams field	Information	Data
Benefit	More than data	Few because they are not processed in the computer
Volume	Tiny	Very large
Source	Limited Source	Multi-source
Order	Regular in a specific structure	irregular in a structure
Accuracy	High	Low
Value	Finite value	Unspecified
location in the system	Output	Input
Use	Used at the official level	Do not use at the official level

Table (1) shows the difference between information and data.

1.3 Definition of data structures.

Data structures are a method or set of laws and regulations to organize data in both secondary and main memory in a computer, so that vocabulary and elements can be dealt with and the relationship between them. That is, they look at the relationship of data among themselves and the relationship of one data structure in another data structure.

Or it can be said that it is the structured formation of a set of data that may share one or more characteristics to serve a specific purpose about a specific thing or set of things. There are many examples, including the following:

1.4 Examples of data structures: -

Example No. (1): If we look at a group of students, we see that each student has a number, name and sign, and if we want to put this data in a list, we can arrange it based on the student's number, name or rate, and we see that these data are related to each other in many things, for example: - The student's name is associated with his number or rate, or the student's association with another to study a course with a professor ... Etc.

If this data is represented in a file, we will see that each student has a set of fields that are related to each other, and bear the characteristic that it is the data of one student only, so it is placed in a record together, and we note that the student's data can be related to the data of another student, the first and second student were in the same group, and we see that the data of the first student is placed in a record and the data of the second student is placed in another record, while these records can be stored together in one file.

- **Conclusion.**

From this example, it is clear that data is interconnected with each other and linked with other data, where we can say that this correlation is placed in a structure such as a file or a list, which is known as data structures.

Example (2): Any telephone directory contains at least two columns, the first column of which is written in the names of individuals, companies or institutions, and the second column contains phone numbers, and we note that these data are arranged alphabetically, to facilitate the search for the name of an individual, institution or company.

Example (3): The names of family members represent a data structure, called or known as tree structures. Where we note that the grandfather can have a group of sons, and that each son can have more than one son, so that the data of this family can be organized in a tree data structure, as shown in the following figure:

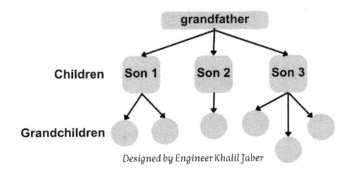

Designed by Engineer Khalil Jaber

Figure (2) shows one of the tree data structures.

Note: There are many examples in our daily lives, which can be expressed using data structures, including but not limited to football team names, which can be organized in a list, flight departure and landing schedules and many more.

2. Benefits of studying data structures.

The study of data structures provides many benefits for students in the field of computer science and software engineering, including:

☐ **Deep understanding of data organization:** The course helps students understand how to organize data in effective ways, enabling them to store and retrieve data quickly and efficiently.

☐ **Improve software performance:** Students can learn how to choose the right data structures for specific tasks, which leads to improved performance of the programs and applications they develop.

☐ **Algorithm analysis:** Understanding data structures helps students analyze the performance of algorithms using concepts such as temporal complexity and spatial complexity, enabling them to write more efficient programs.

☐ **Effective problem solving:** The study of data structures enhances students' problem-solving skills, as they learn how to apply appropriate solutions to different problems using appropriate structures.

☐ **Advanced Subject Preparation:** Data structures are the basis for many advanced courses in computer science, such as analyzing and designing algorithms, databases, and operating systems.

☐ **Advanced Programming Skills:** Students develop advanced programming skills by applying and implementing data structures using different programming languages, enhancing their ability to write clean and structured code.

☐ **Ability to improve existing applications:** Understanding data structures helps students improve existing applications and programs by selecting and implementing more efficient data structures.

☐ **Strong foundation for job interviews:** Understanding data structures is very important for success in job interviews in technology companies, as it is a common topic in which applicants are tested.

☐ **Develop logical and systematic thinking:** The study of data structures contributes to the development of logical and systematic thinking, helping students analyze and solve problems in an organized and effective manner.

3. Types of data structures.

There are many types of data structures that are used for different purposes, and they can be classified into main categories. Here are some common types of data structures:

3.1. Variable data structures.
3.2. Static data structures.

The following diagram shows us the types of data structures and their examples of each.

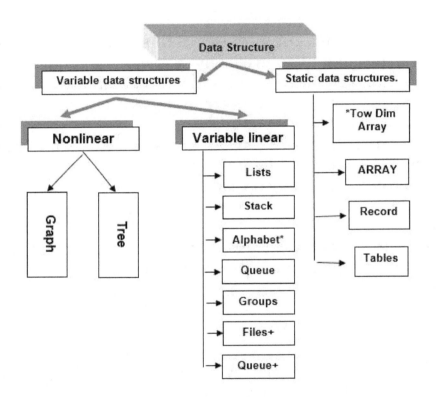

Figure (3) shows all types of data structures.

Note: The data structures next to which the asterisk (*) is located there is a difference in its presence within one group or another, and in general Figure (3) shown earlier will be adopted, and the data structures next to it are (+) to indicate that they have been added within a data structure, and that they are never indicated in many references. In general, it is clear from the previous diagram that the data structures consist of two parts:

3.1 Variable data structures.

They are data structures that change in size, because they accept addition and deletion operations on them, and the number of elements in them can increase or decrease, due to their acceptance of addition and deletion operations, and they are of two types:

3.1.1 linear variable data structures.

These are those structures whose elements are organized in a sequential line, such as files, Stacks, lists, alphabets, queues, groups and disjointed queues.

3.1.2 Nonlinear variable data structures.

They are those variable structures whose elements diverge in more than one direction, such as, trees, maps and Graph.
The following are some examples of variable data structures type I linear and type II nonlinear:

A. Lists.

- Linked Lists.
- Singly Linked List: Nodes can be added and deleted anywhere in the list.
- Singly Linked List: Nodes can be added and deleted anywhere in the list.
- Doubly Linked List: Nodes can be added and deleted from both ends as well as the middle.

- Dynamic Arrays: Like a list in the Python programming language, it can be resized and items can be added and deleted.

B. Queues.

- Regular Queues allow items to be added to the end and removed from the beginning.
- Deque - Double-Ended Queues allow adding and removing items from both ends.

C. Stacks.

Stacks is based on the LIFO principle and allows adding and deleting items from the top of the Stacks.

D. Hash Tables.

Hash tables store data in key/value pairs and allow adding, deleting and modifying values.

E. Trees.

- Binary Search Tree allows you to add, delete and modify nodes.
- The AVL tree is a self-balanced binary search tree that enables modification, deletion, and addition while maintaining balance.
- The B tree is used in databases and allows modification, addition and deletion while maintaining balance.

F. Graphs.

Graphs allow the addition and removal of nodes (anchors) and edges (links) between nodes.

G. Groups (Sets).

Groups (Sets) allow adding and removing items and ensure that items are not duplicated.

H. Tables.

Tables are used in databases and allow adding, deleting and modifying records.

The use of variable data structures depends on the need to modify data frequently and the efficiency of operations related to adding, deleting or modifying elements. These structures offer greater flexibility in handling data, making them suitable for many dynamic and ever-changing applications.

3.2 Static data structures.

These structures consist of a limited set of elements and contain a fixed and fixed number of elements once these structures are created, they cannot be resized.

This means that new items cannot be added or removed, and only existing items can be accessed and modified. These structures are usually used when the number of elements is known in advance and does not change during the implementation of the program. Some common examples of static data structures are:

1. **Array:** A vector is a data structure that stores a fixed number of elements of the same type. Each element can be accessed using a numerical indicator (index).
2. **Fixed-size array:** A type of vector where the vector is resized when it is created and cannot be changed.

3. **Record**: A data structure that can contain elements of different types, but the number and order of these elements is constant.

4. **Fixed group**: A group of elements that can be of different types, and their number and order are fixed.

Static data structures have some advantages such as:

- **High efficiency:** The fixed size makes it easy to manage memory and access items quickly.
- **Easy prediction:** Since the size is constant, the programmer can predict and effectively manage the amount of memory required

However, the limitations of stability make it difficult to use in cases were data size changes frequently, necessitating the use of dynamic data structures such as linked lists or dynamic arrays.

4. Defined operations on data structures.

☐ **Addition**: The addition process can be performed on variable data structures only, and it is forbidden to perform it on fixed data structures, because the number of elements in them is fixed and does not change, and data structures are generally characterized by the possibility of making an addition to any new element.

☐ **Deletion:** It is the second process that can be completed on data structures, especially on variable data structures, where any of their elements can be deleted.

☐ **Integration or Merge**: It is the process of mixing elements of data structures with elements of other data structures to obtain a new data structure, and this process takes place in all types of variable and fixed structures.

☐ **Order**: The elements of data structures can be arranged at many levels, so that they are arranged in ascending or descending order, according to the value of these elements, and the ranking process takes place in all types of data structures.

☐ **Modification (update)**: The values of data structures can be modified or changed, up to a specific date, in all types of data structures.

☐ **Follow-up**: It is the process of searching for one or more elements in data structures, depending on the location of that element, and the value of each element can be known, and this is done in all types of data structures.

5. Data structures Specifications.

Data structures generally share one or more characteristics with each other, and these specifications are: -

☐ Order and value: The one data structure consists of a set of elements, organized in a specific form and a specific order, and if this organization is disturbed, the structure becomes something else, and each element of the data structure has a numeric, literal, symbolic or logical value.
And that the lists are the process of adding and deleting from any side in it, but from the beginning or end, if these operations are limited, for example, from one side only, such as the addition process is from the front only, then the structure of the list data will change to become another structure called the stacks. Data structures can be described by many properties, including order and value. Let me explain both of them:

- Order in data structures refers to how elements are organized in them. Some data structures maintain the order of the elements as entered, while others do not. Let's illustrate this with two examples:

1. Lists: In which the order of the elements is maintained. For example, if you add items in order 1, 2, and 3, they will remain in that order when they are retrieved.

Python example.

```
my_list  = [1,2,3]
print(my_list)  # Output: [1,2,3]
```

2. Sets: In groups, the order of items is not maintained. Items can appear in any order when retrieved.

Python example

```
my_set = {1, 2, 3}
print(my_set)
# Output: {1, 2, 3} (But the order is not guaranteed)
```

- Value: refers to the type of data that can be stored in the data structure and how it is handled. Let's take two examples:

1.Dictionaries: Data can be stored in the form of key-value pairs. The key is used to access the value.

Python example

```
my_dict = {"name": "Alice", "age": 30}
```

```
print(my_dict["name"])  # Output: Alice
```

2.Lists: Stores values based on their positions (indices). You can access the value by using its position in the list.

Python example

```
my_list = [10, 20, 30]
print(my_list[1])  # Output: 20
```

Summary:

- Order: Indicates whether the data structure maintains the order of items as entered.
- Value: Refers to how data is stored and accessed in a data structure, whether using keys, pointers, or no specific order.
- These concepts are fundamental to understanding how to effectively select and use different data structures in programming.

- **Physical structures:** It is considered one of the special specifications that all data share, from the method of storing data on storage media in general or in memory in particular, and we note that there are many methods used to store data on the media for that, and these methods depend on the structure of the data originally and the way it is organized, and in general the method of storage and installation of data in the volume is called physical structures.

   Physical structures in data structures refer to the way in which data is organized in a computer's physical memory. They are about how to allocate memory and how to access data effectively. There are two main types of physical structures: contiguous structures and linked structures. Let me explain each in detail:

A. Contiguous structures in these structures, data is stored in adjacent locations of memory. Examples:

- Arrays.

  - **Description**: An array is a collection of elements of the same type stored in adjacent locations of memory.

  - **Access**: Access to items is fast because the location of any item can be calculated directly through the use of index.

  - **Defects**: Resize the array can be costly in terms of performance as it requires allocating new memory and moving all the elements.

- Text strings:

  - **Description**: A text string is a set of characters stored contiguously in memory.

  - **Access**: Any character can be accessed directly using an index.

  - **Disadvantages**: The same disadvantages as arrays, such as difficulty resizing.

Python example

```python
string = "Hello"
print(string[1])  # Output: e
```

❑ Linked structures in these structures, data is stored in nonadjacent locations of memory, and elements are linked to each other using pointers or links. Examples:

- Description: The linked list consists of nodes, each node containing data and a pointer pointing to the next node.

- Access: To access a specific element, you must navigate through nodes from the beginning until reaching the desired node, which makes access to objects slower compared to arrays.

- Disadvantages: Requires additional space to store indicators.

Python example

```python
class Node:
    def __init__(self, data):
        self.data = data
        self.next = None
class LinkedList:
    def __init__(self):
        self.head = None
    def append(self, data):
        new_node = Node(data)
        if not self.head:
            self.head = new_node
        else:
            current = self.head
            while current.next:
```

```
        current = current.next
    current.next = new_node
```

❑ Trees.

- Description: Trees consist of nodes, where each node contains data and links to child nodes.

- Access: Data can be accessed by navigating through nodes starting at root.

- Disadvantages: It may be complicated in terms of implementation and maintenance.

Python example

```python
class TreeNode:
    def __init__(self, data):
        self.data = data
        self.left = None
        self.right = None
def insert(root, data):
    if root is None:
        return TreeNode(data)
    else:
        if data < root.data:
            root.left = insert(root.left, data)
        else:
            root.right = insert(root.right, data)
        return root
```

Summary:

- Contiguous structures: Like arrays and text strings, they are quick to access elements but have difficulty resizing.

- Linked structures: Like linked lists and trees, they are flexible in size but are slower to access items and require additional space to store pointers.

- Understanding the physical structures of data structures is important to balance performance and flexibility in software design.

❑ **Logical structures:** It is the arrangement of data or information in a sequential and logically organized manner. Logical structures in data structures refer to the way data is organized and arranged from a concept and design point of view, regardless of how it is actually stored in memory.

Logical structures are based on the rules and logic used to organize and process data. There are several types of logic structures, and each type meets certain requirements for different applications. Let's look at some common logical constructs:

- Lists are generally a set of elements that can be homogeneous or heterogeneous, and allow for repetition.

- Linear List: Contains sequentially ordered items, any item can be accessed based on its position.

Python example:

```
my_list = [1, 2, 3, 4, 5]
print(my_list[2])  # Output: 3
```

- Linked List: Contains items called nodes, each node containing data and a pointer to the next node.

Python example:

```python
class Node:
    def __init__(self, data):
        self.data = data
        self.next = None
class LinkedList:
    def __init__(self):
        self.head = None
```

- Stacks: A stack is a data structure that follows the principle of "last income first out" (LIFO - Last In, First Out). Items are added and removed from the same end.

Common operations on stacks.

- 'push': Adds an element to the stack.
- 'pop': Removes the top element from the stack.

Python example:

```python
stack = []
stack.append(1)  # Push
stack.append(2)
print(stack.pop())  # Pop, Output: 2
```

- Queues: A queue is a data structure that follows the principle of (FIFO - First In, First Out). Elements are added from the end and removed from the beginning.

Common operations on queues.

- 'enqueue': Adds an item to the queue.
- 'dequeue': Removes the item from the beginning of the queue.

Python example:

```python
from collections import deque
queue = deque([1, 2, 3])
queue.append(4)  # Enqueue
print(queue.popleft())  # Dequeue, Output: 1
```

- Trees: A tree is a hierarchical data structure consisting of nodes, where each node contains value and links to child nodes. Among the types of trees:

1. Binary Tree: Each node has a maximum of two sub nodes.

Python example:

```python
class TreeNode:
    def __init__(self, data):
        self.data = data
        self.left = None
        self.right = None
```

2. Binary search tree: Each node has a value greater than the values in its left branch and smaller than the values in its right branch.

Python example:

```python
def insert(root, data):
    if root is None:
        return TreeNode(data)
    if data < root.data:
        root.left = insert(root.left, data)
    else:
        root.right = insert(root.right, data)
    return root
```

3. Graphs: They are a set of vertices and edges connecting nodes. Links can be directed or undirected.

Python example:

```python
class Graph:
    def __init__(self):
        self.graph = {}
    def add_edge(self, node, neighbor):
        if node not in self.graph:
            self.graph[node] = []
        self.graph[node].append(neighbor)
```

Summary:

- Logical structures: refers to the way in which data is organized in terms of concept and design.

- Types: Includes lists, stacks, queues, trees, and graphs.

- Important: Helps choose the most appropriate architecture to meet application requirements and improve performance.

Understanding the logical structures of data structures helps in designing effective and flexible solutions to various software problems.

❏ Pointers:

1. Definition of Pointers: It is one of the basic concepts in computer science, and is widely used in data structures and programming, especially in programming languages such as C and C++. A pointer is a variable that stores the memory address of another variable.

2. What are the Pointers?

A Pointers is a variable that stores the location address of another variable. This other variable can be any type of data (e.g. integer, character, data structure, etc.).

3. Uses of Pointers.

- Direct memory access: Through pointers, the contents of the memory can be accessed directly, enabling more effective data manipulation.

- Pass arguments to functions: Pointers can be used to effectively pass arguments to functions, allowing the original values within the function to be modified.

- Dynamic structure management: Pointers are widely used in managing dynamic data structures such as linked lists, trees, and hash tables.

4. Pointers features: flexibility, efficiency and direct access to memory, which accelerates performance. Dealing with dynamic structures will facilitate the construction of complex data structures such as lists and trees.

5. Disadvantages of indicators: Complexity and increased errors in manual memory management may lead to errors such as memory leaks or hanging indicators (Dangling Points). Difficulty learning indicators require a deep understanding of memory and its management, making it difficult to understand for beginners.
6. Disadvantages of Pointers: Complexity and increased errors in manual memory management may lead to errors such as memory leaks or hanging Dangling Pointers. Difficulty learning Pointers require a deep understanding of memory and its management, making it difficult to understand for beginners.

Summary:

Pointers are a powerful and effective programming tool, widely used in data structures and algorithms. Despite its power, it requires good programming and memory management skills to avoid common mistakes. Understanding pointers enhances your ability to write more efficient and flexible programs, and helps you handle dynamic data structures efficiently.

Important Note:

In Python, there are no pointers directly as in languages such as C and C++. Instead, Python relies on object references to manage memory, and this makes things simpler for programmers. Let's explain how to deal with pointers similar concepts in Python:

Definition of variables in Python:

It is a way to store various values such as numbers, text, and other objects. Variables can be thought of as names associated with certain values. Variables in Python are declared very simple, without the need to explicitly specify the data type, as Python determines the type based on the assigned value of the variable.

Example: Suppose A, B are real numbers, how do these variables appear in memory?

In Python, you don't need to declare the type of variables as explicitly as in other programming languages. If we want to deal with it programmatically, it can be declared in a Python program, as follows:

$$a = 0.0$$
$$b = 0.0$$

When executing this sentence, the computer's memory plan is as follows:

$$A \boxed{?}$$
$$B \boxed{?}$$

We note here that variables A and B have been reserved for them in memory in a random way whose address we do not know, even assuming that a value was given to these variables using the following sentences:

$$A = 5.2$$
$$B = 9.5$$

The computer memory diagram after executing these sentences will be as follows:

A	5.2
B	9.5

We can see through this drawing that the variables have retained their values directly, and the computer and through the operating system have determined their address in memory without the user knowing it.

How to declare variables in Python:

To declare a new variable in Python, all you need to do is choose a name for the variable and then use the equal sign (=) to assign a value to it. Here are some examples:

Declaration of an integer variable
```
number = 10
```

Declare a variable for a decimal number
```
float_number = 10.5
```

Text variable declaration
```
text = "Hello, World"!
```

Declare a variable for a list
```
my_list = [1,2,3,4,5]
```

Declare of a variable for a dictionary
```
my_dict = {'name': 'Alice', 'age': 25}
```

Summary:

The programming variables are the elements that take a variable value in the program, and are defined programmatically at the beginning of the program and are defined on one of the data (numeric, literal or symbolic) and store their value in the computer's memory randomly so that these values disappear from memory after the completion of the implementation of the program, and it is not possible to return to it again.

Rules for naming variables.

- Variable names can include letters (a-z, A-Z), numbers (0-9), and underlines (_).
- The variable name must begin with a letter or underscore, and cannot begin with a number.
- Names are case sensitive, which means 'myVariable' and 'myvariable' are different variables.
- It is preferable to use descriptive names to enhance code clarity.

Examples showing how to handle variables in Python.

Use variables in calculations.

```
a = 5
b = 3
sum = a + b
print(sum)  # Output: 8
```

Change variable value.

```
a = 10
print(a)  # Output: 10
```

Use text variables.

```
greeting = "Hello"
name = "Alice"
```

```
message = greeting + ", " + name + "!"
print(message)  # Output: Hello, Alice!
```

These are some simple examples of how to use variables in Python. Variables are mainly considered in programming and are widely used to store and manipulate values in programs.

Now that we know the programming variables, let's get to know the pointers better, let's dive into some key points:

A. What are the Pointers?

A Pointers is an element that locates a variable in a computer's memory and is used in data structures to associate an element with another element and this other variable can be any type of data (e.g. integer, character, data structure, etc.). It has no value since it refers to the value of an element in computer memory and in data structures that we will pointer with an arrow at the tail of which is a small square, as follows:

Pointer

The pointer is distinguished from the software variable in that it has an address in the computer's memory that can be referred to or to the value it refers to even after the end of the implementation of the program.

B. Uses of Pointers:

- Direct access to memory: Through pointers, the contents of memory can be accessed directly, allowing for more effective manipulation of data.

- Pass arguments to functions: Pointers can be used to effectively pass arguments to functions, allowing the original values within the function to be modified.

- Dynamic structure management: Pointers are widely used in managing dynamic data structures such as linked lists, trees, and hash tables.

• Dynamic pointers and data structures

- Linked lists: Each node in the linked list contains a value and pointer for the next node.
- Binary Trees: Each node in the tree contains a value and two pointers, one pointing to the left node and the other to the right node.

• **Advantages and disadvantages of pointers.**

Features:
- Flexibility and efficiency: Provide direct access to memory which accelerates performance.
- Dealing with dynamic structures: Facilitate the construction of complex data structures such as lists and trees.

Defects:
- Complexity and increase of errors: Manual memory management may lead to errors such as memory leaks or hanging pointers.
- Difficulty in learning: pointers require a deep understanding of memory and its management, making it difficult to understand for beginners.

Conclusion:
Pointers are a powerful and effective programming tool, widely used in data structures and algorithms. Despite its power, it requires good programming and memory management skills to avoid common mistakes. Understanding pointers enhances your ability to write more efficient and

flexible programs, and helps you handle dynamic data structures efficiently.

In Python, there are no pointers directly as in languages such as C and C++. Instead, Python relies on object references to manage memory, and this makes things simpler for programmers. Let's explain how to deal with pointers similar concepts in Python:

☐ Object references in Python. Define object references: In Python, variables store object references instead of actual values. This means that variables in Python refer to objects in memory.

☐ Uses of object references. Direct access to objects: Through object references, we can access and modify objects.
☐ Pass arguments to functions: Object references can be passed to functions, allowing the original objects within the function to be modified.
☐ Manage dynamic data structures: Object references can be used to manage dynamic data structures such as linked lists, trees, and dictionaries.

❑ **Operations on object references.**

1. Declare a Python variable.
        var = 10
Here 'var' refers to the object that has the value 10.

2. Reference to another Python object
        another_var = var
  Here 'another_var' refers to the same object as 'var'.

3. Access and modify the object via reference.
        another_var = 20
        print(var)
var remains the same because scalar objects are immutable.

❑ Object references and dynamic data structures.

Linked lists: We can create a linked list using classes in Python.

```python
class Node:
    def __init__(self, data):
        self.data = data
        self.next = None
# Example of creating and linking nodes.
node1 = Node(1)
node2 = Node(2)
node1.next = node2
# Binary Trees: We can create a binary tree using classes.
class TreeNode:
    def __init__(self, data):
        self.data = data
        self.left = None
        self.right = None
    # Example of creating and linking nodes.
root = TreeNode(1)
root.left = TreeNode(2)
root.right = TreeNode(3)
```

Advantages and disadvantages of object references in Python.

Features:

- Ease and simplicity: Memory management is automatic via garbage collection.
- Dynamism and flexibility: Provides high flexibility in dealing with complex data structures.

Disadvantages:

- Performance: In some cases, Python may be slower compared to languages such as C and C++ due to automatic memory management.

– Limited memory control: The inability to manually control memory can be a hindrance in some applications.

Conclusion:

Python simplifies memory management and handling dynamic data structures through object references. While there are no pointers directly in Python, object references provide a powerful and flexible way to manage data and objects in memory. Understanding how object references work can help write more efficient and flexible programs in Python.

– **First Chapter Questions.**

Question 1: Define both:
        A. Data.
        B. Information.
        C. Static data structures.
        D. Variable data structures.

Question 2: Indicate what is the difference between data and information. Or compare data and information.

Question 3: What are the benefits of studying data structures.

Question 4: List the types of data structures.

Question 5: List some non-static data structures.

Question 6: List some non-similar on variable data structures.

Question 7: What is the difference between static and variable data structures. Or compare static and variable data structures.

End of first chapter

Chapter 2:

Variable data structures (linear structures).

1. Lists.
2. Stacks.
3. Queues.
4. Queue Dic.
5. Set (Group).
6. String.
7. Alphabet.
8. Files.

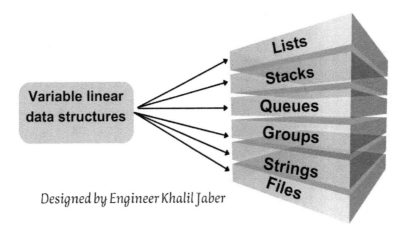

Designed by Engineer Khalil Jaber

❖ **Linear Data Structures.**
1. Lists.

1.1. List Definition:

It is one of the common and widely used data structures in computer science and programming. It is an ordered set of elements, where it can contain duplicates and the elements in it can be accessed by an index. The list can be defined in many programming languages, including:

Define a list in Python.

```
my_list=[1,2,3,4,5]
```

It is a structure of variable linear data structures, and consists of a set of elements, each element of which is called a node, and each element is linked to the next element through an index.

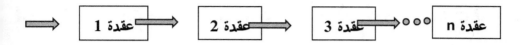

Figure (4) shows the list.

We can see from the previous diagram that the menu items are organized and connected to each other, and have a beginning and an end, and each element in it indicates the next node or the subsequent node.

1.2. Definition of node:

It is the basic unit in the data structure of the linked list type. The node is part of the list, and consists mainly of two elements:

❖ Value: or data carried by the node. This value can be any type of data, such as an integer, text, or other object.

❖ Pointer: Or Link, which is a pointer to the next node in the list. In Singly Linked Lists, this pointer points only to the next node. In Doubly Linked List, there are two pointers, one pointing to the next node and another pointing to the previous node. The following figure shows the node:

Data Fields	Pointer

Figure (5) shows the content of a node from the list.

Example of a node in a one-way linked list in Python:

```
class Node :
def __init__(self, data) :
 self.data=data   #Store data in the node
 #Pointer to the next node, is None when node is created
self.next = None

 #Create two nodes and link them together
Node1=Node(1)
 Node2=node(2)
    Node1.next=node2
#Link the first node to the second node  node1.next=node2
```

The main characteristics of the node in the linked lists are:
- Data: Contains the value of the node.
- Pointers: Contains a reference to the next node in the linked list.

Another example of bidirectional linked lists:

In the bidirectional linked list, each node contains two Pointers: one pointing to the next node and another pointing to the previous node.

```
class DoublyNode :
def __init__(self, data) :
 #Store data in the node
            self.data = data
 #  pointer to next node
            self.next = None
 #Cursor to previous node
            self.prev = None
 # Create two nodes and link them together
      node1 = DoublyNode (1)
```

```
    node2 = DoublyNode(2)
  node1.next = node2
#Link the second node to the first node
    node2.prev = node1
```

Uses:

- Linked one-way list: Used when items are sequentially accessed in one direction only.
- Bidirectional linked menu: used when it is necessary to navigate in both directions (forward and backward).

Nodes are the building blocks of linked lists, and contribute to the flexibility of these structures, such as the ease of adding or removing elements without having to rearrange all items as in arrays.

1.3. Definition of the Data Fields:

The data field is the part of the list that stores data. It contains a specific type of data in the database or spreadsheet. Each field is used to store a specific type of information about the object or record in the list. Lists are a collection of records, and each record contains multiple data fields. For example, in a list that contains information about employees, data fields might include names, addresses, phone numbers, dates of birth, job roles, and so on.

Here's an explanation of some of the concepts related to data fields in lists:
1. Field Name: It is the name given to the field to determine the type of data it contains. For example, "first name", "last name", "date of birth", etc.

2. Data Type: Specifies the type of data that can be stored in the field. Common types include String, Integer, Float, Date, and Boolean.

3. Description: Sometimes the field includes a description that explains the information stored in it and how to use it.

4. Constraints: Conditions or rules imposed on data in a field, such as the field must not be null, the values must be unique, or fall within a certain range.

5. Default Value: A value that is automatically assigned to the field if the user does not provide a certain value when the record is created.

For example, in a spreadsheet for a company's employees, the fields can look like this:

- 'Employee Name': Text data type.
- 'ID number': Data type number.
- 'Date of employment': Date data type.
- 'Salary': Data type number.
- 'Employment status': Text data type.

Each record in this list represents a single employee, and each field provides a piece of information about that employee.

Note: The first node in the list is always a foam and contains a pointer at the beginning known as the Top Pointer and the last node in the list contains a pointer known as the Final pointer or Bottom Pointer.

1.4. Definition of Pointer:

The list pointer is the method used to link list items to each other and is used to refer to the preceding or subsequent node.

A Pointer in the context of lists (especially linked lists) is a variable that stores a memory address for a particular location, usually referring to the next item in the list. Pointers can also point to other elements, such as the previous item or even a specific element in a complex data structure.

To explain this concept in more detail, let's take Linked Lists as an example.

☐ Types of pointers in linked lists:

1. Next Pointer: In Singly Linked List, each item (node) has a pointer pointing to the next node in the list. The last item in the list contains a pointer that points to a special value (often Null) to indicate the end of the list.
2. Previous Pointer: In the Doubly Linked List, each item (node) contains two pointers; one pointing to the next node and the other pointing to the previous node.

Example 1 of a node in a single-linked list in C:

```
struct Node {
        int data;      // data
            struct Node* next;   //   Pointer for next node
};
```

Example 2 of a node in a C-language binary linked list:

```
struct Node {
    int data // data
```

```
    struct Node* next //  ;Pointer for next node
    struct Node* prev //  ;Pointer to previous node
};
```

☐ **Uses**:

- Navigation: With pointers, you can navigate through items in the list effectively.
- Add and delete: Operations on linked lists, such as adding or deleting a node, become easier with pointers without having to rearrange the entire structure like in arrays.

☐ **Benefits**:

- Flexibility: Pointers allow memory management more efficiently and dynamically.
- Memory allocation: Lists associated with the use of pointers can allocate memory to nodes as needed, improving memory utilization.

Overall, pointers are fundamental concepts in data structures, playing a pivotal role in linking data elements and managing memory efficiently.

Lists features:

- Order: Items in the list are stored in a specific order and can be accessed using an index.
- Recurrence: A list can contain duplicate items.

- Diversity: A list can contain different data types (such as integers, text, other lists, etc.).

Basic operations on lists:

☐ Add element: You can add an item to the end of the list using the 'append' function in Python:

```
my_list.append (6)
```

☐ Remove an item: You can remove an item from the list using the 'remove' or 'pop' function in Python :

```
# Remove the item3
my_list.remove (3)
 #Remove the last item in the list
popped_element = my_list.pop()
```

☐ Access an item: You can access an item in the list using the index:

```
#Access the first item in the list
first_element = my_list [0]
```

☐ Edit an item: You can modify the value of a specific item in the list:

```
#Change the value of the first item to 10
my_list[0] = 10
```

Types of lists in programming.

☐ Array Lists: Items are stored in adjacent places in memory, such as lists in Python.

☐ Linked Lists: Each node contains a value and a pointer to the next node. They are divided into:
  - Singly Linked List
  - Doubly Linked List

Lists are flexible and powerful tools that enable programmers to manipulate a range of elements in multiple different ways, making them an essential part of learning programming and data structures.

Example: Illustrates the idea of lists.

If we have a link list containing the names of three students, they are respectively Ahmed, Mohamed, Mahmoud as shown in Figure (6_a) below:

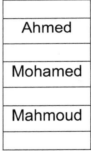

Figure (6_a) A continuous list containing data.

If these names are stored in fictitious locations, we assume them, as shown in figure 6_b.

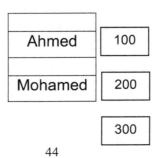

Mahmoud

Figure (6_b) A continuous list containing data and its addresses.

We can use Pointers to refer to the next and previous item for each node in the list [depending on the type of list used] as shown in Figure (6_c) below: -

Ahmed
Nil
Mohamed
100
Mahmoud
200

Figure (6_c) A continuous list containing data and its addresses.

We note from this example that the last node in the list contains the data of the student Mahmoud, and we note that the pointer in it refers to the previous location of him, which is the location 200 in the student Mohamed, and we note that the pointer in the second node refers to the previous location of him, which is the 100 site in the student Ahmed, and according to the example, we see that the first node is not preceded by any other node, and the pointer in it indicates nothing null, To indicate that there is no other data, if we briefly imagine how the representation of this list can be in the computer, we get the following drawing.

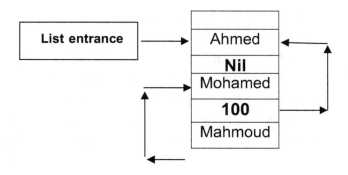

```
┌─────────────┐
│     200     │        ──────────▶
└─────────────┘
```

Figure (7) shows the connected list when following up the data in it.

❏ Types of lists: There are three main types: -

1. Singly Linked Lists.
2. Singly Circular Linked List.
3. Doubly Circular Linked List.

Singly Linked Lists:

(A) Definition of the single connected list:
A single continuous list is a type of linear data structure, consisting of a series of elements, where each element is linked to the next using a pointer or link. Each item in this list is called a node. It contains many nodes, so that these nodes are connected to each other through a pointer, they are called single lists because each node has only one pointer, pointing to the next node, the first node pointer is called the head pointer and the last node pointer points to the Null.

(B) Characteristics of single connected lists:

We note from the previous definition, that it contained important things for this type of list, which is one of the most prominent features of the single connected list, which is characterized by the following characteristics:

1. Each item contains only one pointer, called the Link pointer.
2. The pointer in these lists is only forward (the pointer of each node points only to the next node or the previous one only).
3. The first node is not preceded by anything, and the first node contains a pointer from its beginning called the head pointer.

4. The connection pointer for the last node in this type of list, indicates the Null to indicate the end of the list.
5. Add: A new node can be added to the beginning or end of the list.
6. Delete: A node can be deleted from the beginning or end of the list, or from any specific position.
7. Access: To access a specific item, you must start from the header and go through the nodes until reaching the desired item, which makes the time it takes to reach the item increase with the length of the list.

(C) Single connected list features:

1. Dynamic: It can be easily resized by adding or deleting nodes.
2. Memory usage: More efficient than arrays when it comes to adding or deleting elements, as existing elements do not need to be moved.

(D) Disadvantages of the single connected list:

1. Random Access: No node can be directly accessed. To access a particular node, you must start from the header and pass through the nodes.
2. Pointers: Using pointers can increase the complexity of programming and increase the occurrence of errors.

Single connected list is used in many applications such as dynamic memory management, routing tables in networks, and other applications that require flexible data structure.

Note: The process of representing data in lists varies from type to type, and this difference in the way data is represented is either logical or physical.

Important rule for lists: The data in the list is logically represented by ascending or descending order.

(E) The logical representation of the single continuous list.

Based on the previous definition, the shape of the single connected list will be logically represented as shown in the following figure:

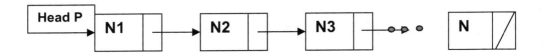

Figure (8) shows the logical representation of the single continuous list.

Example: Shows how to logically represent data in a list.

Let's say we want to logically represent the names of five students, and these names are F, K, Z, A, L, using a single continuous list.

Solution: Based on the previous rule, which stipulates that the data in the list is arranged in ascending or descending order, we put the name of each student inside the node so that the node pointer points to the next node that contains the name of the second student in alphabetical order. And so on. Note that the first node contains the header pointer and the last node contains a pointer indicating (Null) and the shape of this list using this data is represented logically as follows:

Figure (9) shows the logical representation of nouns in a single list.

To create a singly linked list containing the names of five students programmatically using Python, we can define the appropriate objects and functions using Python. We will create a node and a connected list containing basic operations such as adding and displaying.

```python
class Node:
    def __init__(self, data=None):
        self.data = data
        self.next = None
class LinkedList:
    def __init__(self):
        self.head = None
    def append(self, data):
        new_node = Node(data)
        if self.head is None:
            self.head = new_node
            return
        last_node = self.head
        while last_node.next:
            last_node = last_node.next
        last_node.next = new_node
    def display(self):
        current_node = self.head
```

```
            while current_node:
                print(current_node.data, end=" -> ")
                current_node = current_node.next
            print("None")


        # Create a connected list and add student names
        student_list = LinkedList()
        student_names = ["F" ,"K" ,"Z" ,"A" ,"L"]
        for name in student_names:
            student_list.append(name)
        # View connected list
        student_list.display()
```

Code Explanation:

1. We have defined the Node class to represent the node in the connected list. The node contains the data (the name of the student) and the pointer to the next node.

2. We have defined the LinkedList category to represent the connected list. The class contains the header node, ways to add data (append), and display the list.

3. We created a new connected list and added the names of the students using the loop.

4. We displayed the connected list to verify that the names were added correctly.

When the code is executed, the names will appear linked to each other using the arrows to point to the next node.

(F) Physical representation of a single continuous list:

A physical representation of a single continuous list is a way of organizing and storing data so that items are arranged in a sequential manner, but not sequentially in memory.

That is, the physical representation of the data in the single continuous list can be a random order so that the data is distributed in all parts of the list randomly, and it is not a condition that it is contiguous or consecutive, but it is taken into account that each part of these data contains an pointer that physically indicates the next location and therefore we find after passing on all the pointers that the data has been developed according to some order.

There is a vertex pointer that shows where the data begins in the list and there is an end pointer that indicates the blank and the end of the list, and in general the physical representation in the single continuous list is as shown in the following figure:

	100	N2	500

Head	100	N2	500
	200	N5	Nil
300	300	N1	100
	400	N4	200
	500	N3	400

Figure (10) shows the physical representation of single connected lists.

51

Example: Based on the previous example, the data is physically represented in a single continuously list.

Solution: The shape of the list after its physical representation will be as follows: -

	100	F	500
Head	200	Z	Nil
300	300	A	100
	400	L	200
	500	K	400

We notice from the previous drawing that the head pointer shows us where the data begins in the list, and according to our example, we note that the first information is located in the site 300, for example, if we go to that site, we will read the first information in the list, which is the name of the first student A, which is the first names in the list depending on its alphabetical order, then we note that the pointer indicates the site 100, which is the second location in which the second name is stored by alphabet, As we see, this name is the name of the student F, then we see that the pointer indicates the third site, which is 500, which contains the name of the student K, and so the pointers continue to indicate the following sites until we reach the last site in the list, which includes an pointer indicating the blank [Nil] to indicate the end of the list.

The main characteristics of the single connected list.

1. Add Element: A new item is added by creating a new node and adjusting the pointer for the previous node to point to the new node.
2. Delete item: A node is removed from the list by modifying the pointer of the previous node of the node we want to delete to point to the next node after the deleted node.

3. Move between elements: Items are accessed sequentially from the header until reaching the desired node.

This is Python code that shows how to physically represent a single connected list, including basic functions such as adding an item at the beginning of a list, adding an item at the end of the list, and printing the list.

```python
class Node:
    """A class representing a single node in a singly linked list."""

    def __init__(self, data):
        self.data = data  # Holds the data
        self.next = None  # Points to the next node in the list
class SinglyLinkedList:
    """A class representing a singly linked list."""
    def __init__(self):
        self.head = None  # Initialize the head of the list as None
    def append(self, data):
        """Append a new node at the end of the list."""
        new_node = Node(data)
        if self.head is None:
            self.head = new_node
            return
        last_node = self.head
        while last_node.next:
            last_node = last_node.next
        last_node.next = new_node

    def prepend(self, data):
        """Prepend a new node at the beginning of the list."""
        new_node = Node(data)
        new_node.next = self.head
        self.head = new_node

    def print_list(self):
        """Print all the elements in the list."""
        current_node = self.head
        while current_node:
            print(current_node.data, end=" -> ")
            current_node = current_node.next
```

```
    print("None")
```

Example usage:
```
if __name__ == "__main__":
    sll = SinglyLinkedList()
    sll.append(1)
    sll.append(2)
    sll.prepend(0)
    sll.print_list()
```

Explanation of this code in Python:

1. We have defined the Node class to represent the single node in the connected list. This class contains two variables' data for data storage and next for reference storage for the next node.

2. We have defined the SinglyLinkedList class to represent the single connected list. This class contains a head variable that points to the first node in the list.
3. We added append and prepend methods to add new nodes at the end and start of the list respectively.
4. We added a print_list method to print list items.

When you run the program, a single concatenated list will be created containing items 0->1->2.

Exercise 1: Suppose we have logically represented data in the following single continuous list:

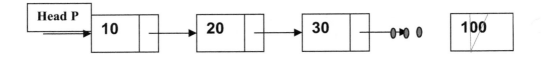

This data is required to be physically represented in a single continuous list.

Solution:

1	100	Nil
2	30	7
3	10	5
4	60	8
5	20	2
6	80	10
7	40	9
8	70	6
9	50	4
10	90	1

Head 3

HEAD 3

Exercise 2: From the following list physically represented.

1	C	6
2	E	5
3	G	Nil
4	A	7
5	F	3
6	D	2
7	B	1

4

Required: Logically represent the data in the previous list.

Solution:

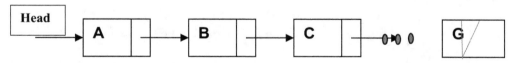

Exercise 3: If we have the following list, which includes the names of five students and their averages.

NASER	95
ALI	90
ZIAD	80
YASER	45
SALEM	30

Asks: I work on representing this data logically and physically, taking into account that the order of the data is in ascending order based on student averages only:

Solution:

1	YASIR	95	Null
2	SALEM	30	5
3	ALI	90	1
4	ZIAD	80	3
5	NASER	50	4

2

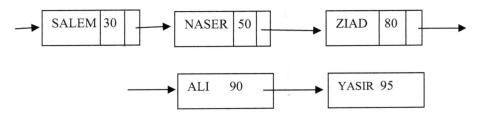

SALEM	30	→	NASER	50	→	ZIAD	80	→

→	ALI	90	→	YASIR	95

Circular Linked Lists:

It is a type of graph that looks like linked lists, but with the fundamental difference that the last element in the circular list refers to the first element, making it circular. A circular list can be defined as follows:

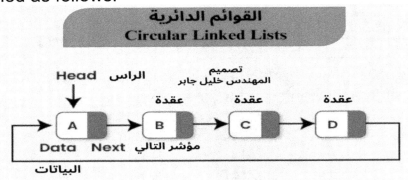

القوائم الدائرية
Circular Linked Lists

تصميم
المهندس خليل جابر

Head الرأس   عقدة   عقدة   عقدة

A → B → C → D

Data   Next   مؤشر التالي

البيانات

Figure (11) shows the logical representation of the circular list of contact.

Main characteristics: Each node contains data and a Pointer point to the next node. The last node refers to the first node, creating a circular loop.

Types of circular lists:
(A) Singly Circular Linked List:

Each node has only one pointer pointed to the next node. The last node contains a pointer pointing to the first node.

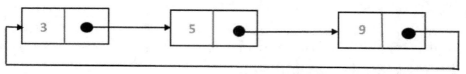

Figure (12) shows the logical representation of the single-connected circular list.

(B) Doubly Circular Linked List:

Each node contains two pointers, one pointing to the next node and another pointing to the previous node. The last node refers to the first node, and the first node points to the last node.

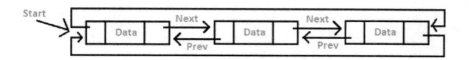

Figure (13) shows the logical representation of a circular double-connected list.

Note: The single circular linked list is used to represent the circular linked list.

1. Represent the circular linked list using Python.

Circular linked lists are similar to individual linked lists except that the last node is connected to the first node.

```
#Class Node, similar to the linked list
class Node:
    def __init__(self,data):
        self.data = data
        self.next = None
```

Example of a single circular linked list:

From the previous figure number (12), the single circular list can be represented as follows.

```
#Initialize the Nodes.
one = Node(3)
two = Node(5)
three = Node(9)
#Connect nodes
one.next = two
two.next = three
three.next = one
```

Benefits and Uses:

− Efficient rotation: Rotate through items continuously without having to reach the end of the list and start over.

- Easy to add and remove: Items can be added or removed anywhere in the list without having to relink multiple nodes.

- Use in periodic applications: such as schedules or games where the continuous implementation of a specific cycle of operations is required.

Basic operations:

- Insertion: A new item can be added at the beginning and end of a list, or at a specific location.
- Deletion: An item can be deleted from the beginning, end, or from a specific location.
- Search: A specific item can be searched by navigating through the contract.
- Display: Displays all list items starting from the first node.

An example of creating a single-link circular list:

```
class Node:
    def __init__(self, data):
        self.data = data
        self.next = None

class CircularLinkedList:
    def __init__(self):
        self.head = None

    def append(self, data):
        new_node = Node(data)
        if not self.head:
            self.head = new_node
            self.head.next = self.head
        else:
            temp = self.head
```

```python
            while temp.next != self.head:
                temp = temp.next
            temp.next = new_node
            new_node.next = self.head

    def display(self):
        nodes[] =
        temp = self.head
        if self.head:
            while True:
                nodes.append(temp.data)
                temp = temp.next
                if temp == self.head:
                    break
        print(" -> ".join(map(str, nodes)))

# Create a circular list and add items.

cll = CircularLinkedList()
cll.append(1)
cll.append(2)
cll.append(3)
cll.display()  # Output: 1 -> 2 -> 3
```

With this example, we created a single-connected circular list, added some items to it, and then displayed its contents.

Advantages of circular linked lists:

- Any node can be the starting point. We can also traverse the entire list by starting from any point. And we only need to stop when visiting the first node visited again.
- They are useful for queue execution. Unlike implementation, we don't need to hold forward and backward pointer if we use a circular linked list. We can hold a pointer to the last

node that was inserted and the foreground can always be obtained as the next node of the last node.

- Circular lists are useful in apps to navigate around the list frequently. For example, when running multiple applications on a computer, it is common for the operating system to put running applications in a list and then navigate between them, giving each a slice of time to execute, and then making them wait while the CPU is given to another application. It is convenient for the operating system to use a circular list so that it can navigate to the front of the list when it reaches the end of the list.
- Double-linked circular lists are used to implement advanced data structures.
- Implementing a circular linked list can be relatively easy compared to other, more complex data structures such as trees or graphs.

Disadvantages of the circular linked lists:

- Compared to individually linked lists, circular lists are more complex.
- Inverting a circular list is more complex than reversing a circular list individually or doubly.
- It is possible that the code will enter into an infinite loop if not handled carefully.
- It's hard to find the end of the list and control the loop.
- Although circular linked lists can be effective in some applications, their performance can be slower than other data structures in certain situations, such as when the list needs to be sorted or searched.
- Circular linked lists don't provide direct access to individual nodes.

Applications of circular linked lists:

- Multiplayer games use this to give every player a chance to play.
- The circular linked list can be used to organize several applications running on the operating system. These applications are duplicated by the operating system.
- Circular linked lists can be used in resource allocation problems.
- Circular linked lists are commonly used to implement circular buffers,
- Circular linked lists can be used in simulations and games.

Why a linked list circular?

Finally, here's a simple Python example that shows how to create and manage a single online list:

```python
class Node:
    def __init__(self, data):
        self.data = data
        self.next = None

class SinglyLinkedList:
    def __init__(self):
        self.head = None

    def append(self, data):
        new_node = Node(data)
        if not self.head:
            self.head = new_node
            return
        last = self.head
        while last.next:
            last = last.next
        last.next = new_node

    def print_list(self):
```

```python
        current = self.head
        while current:
            print(current.data, end=" -> ")
            current = current.next
        print("None")
```

Create a single connected list and add some items

```python
sll = SinglyLinkedList()
sll.append(1)
sll.append(2)
sll.append(3)
sll.print_list()
```

Questions:

Question 1: Define both:
1. Data.
2. Information.
3. Lists.
4. Node.
5. Pointers.
6. The logical structure of the list.
7. The physical structure of the list.

Question 2: Explain the concept of physical structure.

Question 3: Explain the concept of logical structure.

Question 4: I make a comparison between static data structures and variable data structures.

Question 5: What are the processes defined on data structures? Explain one of them.

Question 6: What are the specifications of data structures? With explanation.

Question 7: What is the difference between static data structures and variable data structures.

Question 8: Where are the following operations carried out, and in what type of data structure?
1. Addendum.
2. Deletion.
3. Merge.

Question 9: Why are linear structures so named?

Question 10: What are the stages that data goes through to become information?

Question 11: What is the difference between data and information?

Question 12: I make a comparison between data and information.

Question 13: What is the difference between a physical representation and a logical representation in a single continuous list?

2.1. Definition of stacks.

It is a structure of variable linear data structures consisting of one or more elements in which elements are placed one by one and on top of each other. A stack can be likened to a set of stacked books, where books are added to the top of the pile and also removed from the top.

The first element is referred to by a pointer called the bottom pointer and the last element is referred to as a pointer called the top pointer of the top stack, and the stack is characterized by allowing the process of adding and deleting from one side only, specifically from the top, and uses in its work the principle of the Last In the First Out (LIFO) and the following figure shows the stack:

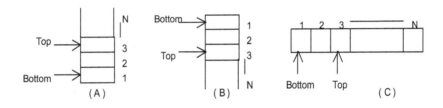

Figure (14) shows the STACKS physically .

2.2. Basic operations in the Stack.

• Push: Add an element to the top of the stack.
• Pop: Remove and return the item at the top of the stack.
• Peek/Top: Returns the item at the top of the stack without removing it.
• isEmpty: Check if the stack is empty.
• Size: Returns the number of items in the stack.

The stack consists of a group of elements placed on top of each other so that the first element at the bottom of the stack is indicated by the bottom pointer and the last element at the top of the stack is referred to as the Top pointer and the previous graphics theoretically show how to draw the stack and show the physical locations in the computer memory in which the data is stored, as it is clear to us from the previous figure that the stack can contain only one element and in this case the bottom pointer and the top pointer of the top of the stack indicate the same element, i.e. that top=Bottom.

The stack can also contain more than one element that may number up to N items, and we must know that the Top pointer moves with the data so that it always indicates the last element in the stack and when performing any operation to add it to the stack, we are working to add one to the value of the Top pointer using the following equation

$$Top=Top+1$$

In order for this pointer to move and point to the new added element, if any deletion is made in the stack, we decrease one of the Top pointers using the following equation:

$$Top=Top-1$$

Until the pointer points to the last element in the stack, in this way we can add or delete from the package but using the LIFO principle.

2.3. The principle of Last In First Out (LIFO).

Stack uses this principle in its work because it accepts addition and deletion from one point only, which is from the top, so we see when adding more than one element in the stack, the first element in it is in the first position, that is, it is at the bottom of the stack, and the second element comes directly above it, then the third element above it, and so on.

When you want to retrieve or delete an item from the stack, we can only do so from the top of the stack, which usually contains the last item, and this process is similar to the process of placing a group of books on top of each other, assuming that there are ten books inside a box as follows:

So the first book is at the bottom of the box and the last book is at the top of the box, if we want, for example, to take out book number five from the box, we must take out all the books above, starting with book number ten, then book number nine, and so on until we reach book number five, and in this case we can say that book number ten last is inside the box and the first to get out of it. To illustrate the LIFO principle well, let's see the following example:

Example: Demonstrates the LIFO principle and the addition principle in Stack.

Suppose we have the letter A, B, C, D and want to enter it into the Stack, we use the following steps:

(A) At first, the stack is an empty and a top pointer and a bottom pointer indicate the bottom of the stack and the value of each is zero, and when the first letter A is added to the stack, the Top pointer takes a value that increases by one using the equation Top=Top+1 The shape of the stack becomes as follows:

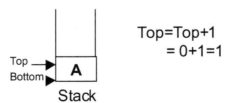

$$Top=Top+1$$
$$= 0+1=1$$

Stack

Figure (15) shows the stack after adding the first item.

(B) The second letter B is entered on the Stack and placed over the first letter with the Top pointer position moved to point to the new item B and the stack becomes as follows:

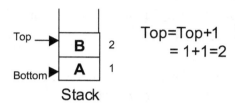

Figure (16) shows the package after adding the second item.

(C) The third letter C is entered in the same way as the previous one and the Stack shape becomes as follows:

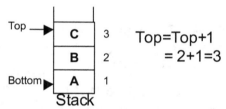

Figure (17) shows the package after adding the third element.

(D) The last letter D is entered into the stack with the top pointer modified as follows:

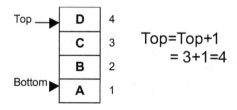

Figure (18) shows the package after adding the last item.

We note from the previous steps that we performed the addition process on Stack in order and from the top side only, starting from the first element, which is the letter A, which is now at the bottom of the stack, and ending with the last element, which is the letter D, which is located at the top of the stack, and this process is called the process of pushing the elements inside the stack Push and the stack is now in which all the required literal data, if we now want to take out the first element from the Stack.

We must take out all the other elements above it, provided that we start taking out the inside element last, which is the letter D at the top of the stack, then the next element, and so on until we reach the desired element, which is the letter A, and this method is called the principle of finally inside out first LIFO, which is the same method we use to pull elements from Stack.

2.4. The process of **pulling elements from Stack** using the LIFO principle.

This process is called the process of dragging and retrieving elements from the POP stack, and the stack in this case is full and the Top pointer in it indicates the last element, and the Bottom pointer indicates the bottom of the stack and its value is equal to zero, so if we now want to take out the letter A entering first to the stack, we must take out all the other letters above it, and provided that we start taking out the letter D entering finally at the top of the stack and then the letter C that follows it and so on until we reach the letter A and to do that, we use the following steps:

(a) The last letter D is pulled from the stack and the pointer Top takes a value that decreases by one by using the equation Top=Top-1 The shape of the stack becomes as follows:

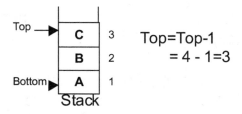

$$\text{Top} = \text{Top} - 1$$
$$= 4 - 1 = 3$$

Figure (19) shows the stack after the last element is drawn.

(b) The next letter, the letter C, is dragged from the Stack with the Top pointer position moved to point to the letter B and the stack reads as follows:

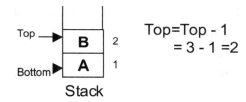

$$\text{Top} = \text{Top} - 1$$
$$= 3 - 1 = 2$$

Figure (20) shows the stack after the third element is withdrawn.

(c) The letter B is dragged in the same style as the previous one and the Stack shape becomes as follows:

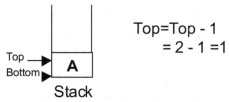

$$\text{Top} = \text{Top} - 1$$
$$= 2 - 1 = 1$$

Figure (21) shows the stack after the second element is withdrawn.

(d) We now notice that we have reached the desired character but after we have dragged all the other characters from the Stack that were on top of it.

2.5. Stack features.

Stack is used a lot in computers because it has many important features, including the following:

☐ Stack uses a very small part of the computer's memory.
☐ The stack accepts the process of adding and deleting from one side only, which is from the top, and this feature is used by using Stack in the process of calling subprograms.
☐ The stack works with the principle of LIFO in addition and deletion operations.
☐ Stack has only one pointer that always indicates the last item from the top and is called the Top pointer.
☐ The process of adding items to the stack is called PUSH and the process of dragging or canceling items from the stack is called POP. The item at the top of the stack can be returned without removing it.
☐ Stack can be used to perform addition, subtraction, multiplication, division.
☐ Every element in the Stack has a predecessor and successor except the first element that does not have a preceding element and the last element that does not have a suffix.

2.6. How to represent Stack programmatically.

Stack can be represented programmatically using many methods, the most important of which is to represent the stack by a continuous list or by array.

Method 1: Represent Stack programmatically by list.

After we studied in the previous chapters how to represent the list programmatically, it is now easy for us to represent the Stack through the list, but taking into account that the stack differs from the list in the way data is entered into it and that it only accepts the addition and deletion operations from one side. In practice, the representation of the stack through the list is used to implement programs very quickly because they reserve a small part of the computer's memory, and to clarify the principle of representing the stack through the list, let's take the following example:

Example: Demonstrates how to represent Stack through the list.
Suppose we have literals A, B, C, D, and E stored inside Stack as follows:

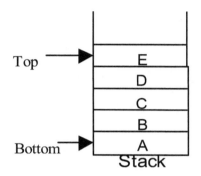

Figure (22) shows literal data represented in a stack.

If we look at this stack well, we find that it is a continuous list, and we can draw it through the list as follows:

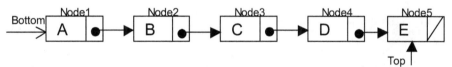

Figure (23) shows how the stack is represented through the list.

We note through the previous drawing that the stack represented by the list contains a starting pointer Bottom indicates the beginning of the list and the end pointer of the last node indicates the void Null and all other nodes refer to each other, and this list is distinguished from the lists The other one we studied earlier with the Top pointer, which always points to the last element in it, and this means limiting the addition and deletion process from one side only. Now that we know the details of this list, let's see how to program this stack through the list.

Stack representation program through the list using Python.

```python
class StackElement:
    def __init__(self, data):
        self.data = data
        self.link = None

class Stack:
    def __init__(self):
        self.top = None

    def push(self, data_item):
        new_element = StackElement(data_item)
        new_element.link = self.top
        self.top = new_element

    def pop(self):
        if self.top is None:
            print('Stack is empty')
        else:
            temp = self.top
            self.top = self.top.link
            print(f'Item removed from stack is {temp.data}')

    def list_stack(self):
        print('----------')
        current = self.top
        while current is not None:
            print(current.data)
            current = current.link
        print('----------')

def main():
    stack = Stack()
    menu_line = 'Action (1 = Push, 2 = Pop, 3 = Quit) ? '
    prompt = 'Enter data item '

    while True:
        choice = int(input(menu_line))
        if choice == 1:
            data_item = input(prompt)
```

```python
            stack.push(data_item)
            stack.list_stack()
        elif choice == 2:
            stack.pop()
            stack.list_stack()
        elif choice == 3:
            print('Program terminated')
            break
        else:
            print('Invalid action')

if __name__ == "__main__":
    main()
```

Explain the Stack impersonation program through the list using Python.

At the beginning of the program, we defined the elements and the stack. Define StackElement to contain the data and link fields. and the definition of Stack and push, pop, and list_stack actions. And stack procedures:

1. Push add an item to the stack.
2. Pop remove an item from the stack and view it.
3. list_stack display the contents of the stack.

The main program in Python.

we use a while loop to repeat the user's input until he chooses to exit. We handle inputs and actions based on the user's choice.

We note from the previous program that we advertise the Stack at the beginning of the program as if it were a list using pointers and record, and we used the first procedure PUSH to enter data into the Stack in the same way as entering data to the list, but from the top side only, and we used the second procedure POP to delete items from Stack

But note that this procedure does not allow the deletion process for any element from the Stack, but the deletion process is restricted from the top only, and we have used a third procedure list_stack to display the content of the stack on the screen after completing each process, and finally we used a main program in which a conditional repetition sentence while in order to perform one of the actions as desired.

Method 2: Represent Stack programmatically by an array.
Stack can be represented by a one-dimensional Array as the elements in Stack are stored in it one after another as in a vector, and the element in the vector is defined by locating it in the vector, and the following example shows us this.

Example: Shows how to represent Stack through the one-dimensional Array.
If we go back to Stack in the previous example, which contained the character set A, B, C, D, E, it shows us as follows:

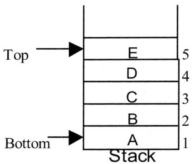

Figure (24) shows a stack containing literal data.

Now if we look at it well, we find that this stack can be seen as a five-element one-dimensional Array, for example we named this Array XY then this Array would be as follows:

	xy[1]	xy[2]	xy[3]	xy[4]	xy[5]
XY	A	B	C	D	E

Figure (25) shows how stack is represented by an array.

Now this stack can be represented programmatically by an XY array and its number of elements is five using the following steps:

1. Array definition: In Python, an array can be defined using lists. Here, XY is a list of length 5.

2. Push function: The push function receives the top value and adds a new element to the Stack if it is not full.

3. POP function: The POP function receives the top value and removes the top item from the stack if it is not empty. A condition in this procedure linked to the TOP variable is used to stop printing, when the Top value becomes zero.

4. A decreasing value is given by one to the variable Top in order to output the Stack elements one by one and from the top, and when the amount of Top becomes zero, the process of ejecting the Stack elements ends and becomes Stack Empty of all elements.

5. Main program: uses For loops to call push and pop functions.

Note:

Make sure the program is running in an environment that supports user input via input() in Python, and experiment with character input to make sure it works correctly.

6. We write a main program in which one spin loop is called the first action Push to read the stack elements, and then we use another single spin loop in which the second action is called Pop to print the stack elements.

Finally, the Python program representing the stack by the Array XY becomes as follows:

```python
# This is a demo program to implement a stack using an array in Python
# Initialize the stack with a fixed size
XY = ['''] * 5
top = 0
def push(top):
    global XY
    if top >= 5:
        print('Stack Full')
    else:
        character = input(f'Enter ({top + 1}) Character: ')
        XY[top] = character
        top += 1
    return top
def pop(top):
    global XY
    if top == 0:
        print('Stack Is Empty')
    else:
        top -= 1
        print(XY[top])
    return top
# Main Program
for i in range(5):
```

```
    top = push(top)
print('\n\nList Content of the stack')
print('-------------------------')
for i in range(5):
    top = pop(top)
```

Applications of Stacks.

Stack is used in many important software applications, and its most important uses are:

A. Finding the values of arithmetic expressions with the formulas Postfix, Prefix.

B. Stack is used to call subprograms and execute traps.

C. Stack is used in the Recursion self-recall process.

D. Let us now examine these applications in detail.

2.7. Find the values of arithmetic expressions with the formulas Postfix, Prefix.

The stack is of great importance in finding the values of arithmetic expressions and works to find the value of any arithmetic expression written in Infix format by converting it to Postfix or Prefix formula, but how does this process work? And what are these formulas?

☐ **Infix format**. This formula is called the middle formula, and as it is known to us that all arithmetic expressions usually consist of variables or constants or both together and are separated by the signs of arithmetic operations such as the addition sign (+) or subtraction (-) or multiplication (*) or division (/), and in the Infix formula we find that the arithmetic expression in which the sign of the arithmetic operation is placed in the middle between variables and constants, if we look at the following arithmetic expression: X + Y

We find that the variable X represents the left term and the variable Y represents the right term in the arithmetic expression, and we also find that the plus sign (+) is written in the middle of the terms, and we can say that this formula is called the Infix formula, which is the usual mathematical formula used in mathematics, in which the sign of the arithmetic operation is always written in the middle of the term according to the following law:

Right Limit – Calculation Signal – Left Term

☐ **Prefix formula.** This formula is called the "tribal formula" because the sign of the arithmetic operation precedes the variables and constants, and the arithmetic expression is written in Prefix form as follows:

Left Limit – Right Limit – Calculation Signal

Example: The arithmetic expression X+Y can be written using the Prefix formula as follows: XY+

We can see from this formula that the sign of the addition calculation (+) preceded the variables.

☐ **Postfix formula**. This formula is called the "dimensional formula", which means that we write the sign of the arithmetic operation in the arithmetic expression after variables and constants as shown in the following formula:

Calculation Signal - Left Limit – Right Limit

Example: The preceding arithmetic expression X+Y is written using the Prefix formula as follows: +XY

We note here how the sign of the arithmetic operation addition (+) was written after the variables.

Now let's go back to Stack and see how it works to find the values of arithmetic expressions? Usually, the arithmetic expression is written in the regular mathematical formula Infix and this formula is converted to Prefix or Postfix form using the method of linking signs to parentheses, and then the values of the arithmetic expression are entered into Stack, as we will see later.

The principle of associating signs with parentheses to transform mathematical formulas.

This method is used to convert the arithmetic expression written in Infix format to any other formula such as Postfix or Prefix, and this method is generally summarized by limiting each pair of variables or constants in parentheses with the reference of the arithmetic operation, and these parentheses are placed using the priorities of the calculations used in the computer, The number of parentheses on the right side in the arithmetic expression must be equal to the number of parentheses on the left side and equal to the number of signs of arithmetic operations, after that the parentheses are changed with the signs of arithmetic operations from the right or left, according to the formula to which we want to convert, as shown in the following:

How to convert an arithmetic expression from Infix formula to Postfix formula.

Converting an Infix arithmetic expression to Postfix is done using the principle of associating signs with parentheses, as shown in the following steps:

❏ The parentheses are placed in the Infix formula using the priorities of calculations, provided that inside each parenthesis there is only one right limit and one arithmetic sign in addition to the left term, and the number of parentheses in each arithmetic expression on the right side is equal to the number of parentheses on the left side and equal to the number of calculation signals.

❏ All parentheses are removed from the left in the arithmetic expression.

❏ Now the signal of each calculation is linked to only one parenthesis from the right, provided that it does not intersect with each other.

❏ Each parenthesis on the right is replaced by the associated calculation signal.

For example, after converting an A+B expression written in Infix format to Postfix format, AB+

To illustrate the previous points, let us take the following example:

Example: Demonstrates the principle of converting an arithmetic expression from Infix to Postfix formula.

Suppose we want to convert the Infix expression to the following Postfix formula:

$$(A+B) / (C+D+E) +5 \quad \Rightarrow \textit{Infix}$$

We use the principle of associating signals with parentheses as follows:

A. The parentheses on the arithmetic expression shall be placed according to the priorities of the calculations, as follows:

$$(((A+B) / ((C+D) + E)) + 5)$$

The priorities of calculations in arithmetic expressions are generally as follows:

- Confined operations are carried out within parentheses and according to priorities.

- The division and multiplication process have the same rank in execution, if the two operations occur together in the arithmetic expression, the one that falls on the left is executed first.

- The addition and subtraction process also have the same rank in implementation, if the two operations occur together in the arithmetic expression, the one that falls on the left is executed first.

Now that we have finished placing the parentheses on the previous arithmetic expression according to the priorities of the calculations, we notice that the number of parentheses on the right side is equal to the number of parentheses on the left side and is equal to the number of signs of arithmetic operations.

B. Leave the brackets on the right side and remove all the brackets on the left, as follows:

$$A+B) / C+D) + E)) + 5)$$

C. Calculation signals are now linked to parentheses from the right, as follows:

$$\text{A+B)/C+D\textbf{)} + E) \textbf{)} + 5 \textbf{)}}$$

D. Finally, the parentheses on the right are replaced with the associated calculation signs, and we have the following Postfix formula:

AB + CD + E +/ 5+ ⇨ **Postfix**

We note here after replacing parentheses with arithmetic operations flags, they are permanently removed from the arithmetic expression and you should write the Postfix formula without parentheses.

Another example. Using the principle of linking signs to parentheses, convert the Infix arithmetic expression to the following Postfix formula:

(A*B) + (A−B) / (2*A) ⇨ **Infix**

This arithmetic expression can be converted from Infix to Postfix form using the principle of associating signs with parentheses, as follows:

- Brackets are placed on the arithmetic expression according to the priorities of the calculations.

((A*B) + ((A−B) / (2*A))) ⇨ **Infix**

- All parentheses are removed from the left, as follows:

$$A*B) + A-B) / 2*A))) \quad \Rightarrow \text{Infix}$$

- Now the signs of the calculations are connected to the parentheses from the right with the note that none of them intersect, as follows:

$$A * B) + A - B) / 2 * A)))$$

- Finally, the parentheses on the right are replaced with the associated calculation signals and thus we have the following Postfix formula:

$$AB * AB - 2A * / + \quad \Rightarrow \text{Postfix}$$

How to convert an arithmetic expression from Infix formula to Prefix formula.

An arithmetic expression written in Infix form can be converted to Prefix form using the principle of associating the signs of arithmetic operations with parentheses, and this process is done as follows:

- The parentheses are placed in the Infix formula using the priorities of calculations, provided that inside each parenthesis there is only one right limit and one arithmetic sign in addition to the left term, and the number of parentheses in each arithmetic expression on the right side is equal to the number of parentheses on the left side and equal to the number of calculation signals.

- All parentheses are removed from the right in the arithmetic expression.

- Now the sign of each calculation is linked with only one arc on the left, noting that it does not intersect with each other.

- Each parenthesis on the left is replaced by the associated calculation signal. In this way, we have obtained the Prefix formula.

For example, to convert the expression A+B from Infix to Prefix, we perform the previous four points and then obtain the following formula: +**AB**

Example: Demonstrates the principle of converting an arithmetic expression from Infix to Prefix formula.

$$(A+B) \; / \; (C+D+E) \; +5 \quad \Rightarrow \textit{Infix}$$

To convert the previous arithmetic expression written in Infix form to Prefix form using the principle of associating the signs of calculations with parentheses, we perform the following steps:

- Brackets are placed on the arithmetic expression according to the priorities of the calculations.

$$((\;(\;A+B\;)\;/\;(\;(\;C+D\;)\;+\;E\;)\;)\;+\;5\;)\quad \Rightarrow \text{Infix}$$

- All parentheses are removed from the right, as follows:

$$((\ (\ A+B\ /\ (\ (\ C+D\ +\ E\ +\ 5 \qquad \Rightarrow \textbf{Infix}$$

- The signs of calculations are linked to the parentheses on the left, noting that none of them intersect, as follows:

- Now the parentheses on the left are replaced with the associated calculation signals and we have the following Prefix formula:

$$+\ /\ +\ \textbf{AB}\ +\ +\ \textbf{C\ D\ E\ 5} \qquad \Rightarrow \textbf{Prefix}$$

☐ Use the stack directly to find the values of arithmetic expressions.

Now that we have learned about the principle of associating signs with parentheses and how to convert an arithmetic expression from one formula to another, let's now see how the stack works to find the values of arithmetic expressions.

In the beginning, the arithmetic expression is converted from the Infix formula to one of the formulas that we explained earlier (Postfix formula or Prefix formula), then we work to read the arithmetic expression using the Push operation and the Pop operation, when reading a variable or constant, we use the push process, which means pushing the variable or constant into the stack, but in the case of passing while reading the arithmetic expression with the sign of the calculation itself, we use the POP withdrawal process, which means the implementation of this operation within the stack And from above, Specifically, the calculation is performed only at the top of the stack between the location indicated by the Top pointer and the site preceding it known as Top-1 in which the result is stored, and we use in the stack instead of the calculation signals the following:

☐ Instead of addition signs (+) we use the word Add.
☐ Instead of subtraction signs (-) we use the word Subtract.
☐ Instead of multiplication signs (*) we use the word Multiply.
☐ Instead of division signs (/) we use the word divide.

Let's now see how the process of reading and finding the values of arithmetic expressions works.

How to read and find the values of arithmetic expressions in Postfix form using Stack.

The value of an arithmetic expression in Postfix form is found by reading this expression from the left towards the right, and when passing a variable or constant, we push it into the stack using the word Push, and when reading the sign of the calculation, we use the word pop and then execute it inside the stack, and the following examples show us this.

Example 1. Using the stack, find the result of the arithmetic expression written in the following Infix form:

$$(A \ / \ C) + (D \ * \ 2) \ \textbf{Infix}$$

Solution: To evaluate this expression using Stack, we convert it to Postfix formula using the principle of associating signs with parentheses, and then we get the following formula:

AC / D2 * + Postfix

Then we read this expression from left to right using push and pop operations and thus get the following operations:

Push A	This process pushes element A into the stack
Push C	This process pushes element C into the stack
Pop	Perform the calculation.
Divide	Division process.
Push D	This process pushes element D into the stack.
Push 2	This process pushes item 2 into the stack.
Pop	Perform the calculation.
Multiply	Multiplication process.
Pop	Perform the calculation.
Add	Collection process.

Now we are working on representing the arithmetic expression within the stack using the following steps:

Top → [A] Push A	(1)The Push A operation is performed, that is, we push element A inside the stack as shown in the drawing.
Top → [C] 2 Bottom → [A] 1 Push C	(2)The operation performs Push C and the stack becomes as follows

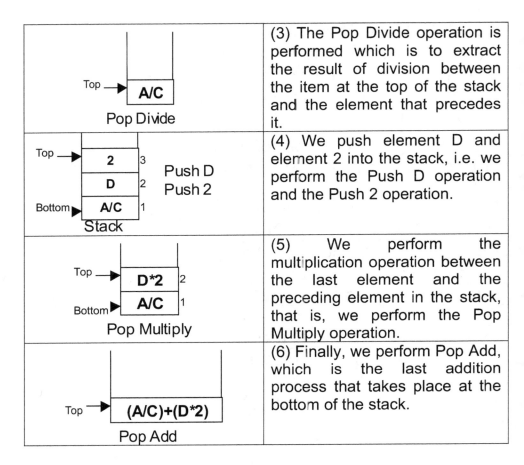

Top → A/C Pop Divide	(3) The Pop Divide operation is performed which is to extract the result of division between the item at the top of the stack and the element that precedes it.
Top → 2 |3 D |2 Bottom ► A/C |1 Stack	(4) We push element D and element 2 into the stack, i.e. we perform the Push D operation and the Push 2 operation. Push D Push 2
Top → D*2 |2 Bottom ► A/C |1 Pop Multiply	(5) We perform the multiplication operation between the last element and the preceding element in the stack, that is, we perform the Pop Multiply operation.
Top → (A/C)+(D*2) Pop Add	(6) Finally, we perform Pop Add, which is the last addition process that takes place at the bottom of the stack.

So, we've got the final arithmetic expression value within the stack. For example, if we assume that the value of A=10, the value of C=2, and the value of D=3, the value of the previous arithmetic expression using the stack becomes as follows:

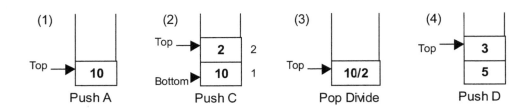

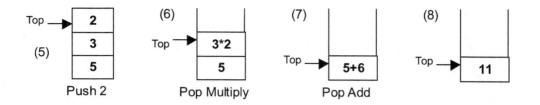

Figure (26) Finding the value of an arithmetic expression using Stack.

Example 2: Using the stack find the result of the following arithmetic expression:

$$(A+20) / (A-B-C) * 2$$

If you know that the value of A=10, the value of B=2, and the value of C=3.

Solution: The expression is converted from Infix to Postfix form using the principle of associating signs with parentheses, so we get the following formula:

$$A20 + AB - C - / 2 *$$

This expression is read using the Push process and the Pop operation and from the left to the right.

Push A

Push 20

Pop

Add

Push A

91

Push B

Pop

Sub

Push C

Pop

Sub

Pop

Div

Push 2

Pop

Multiply

We now use the stack to evaluate the arithmetic expression as shown in the following diagram:

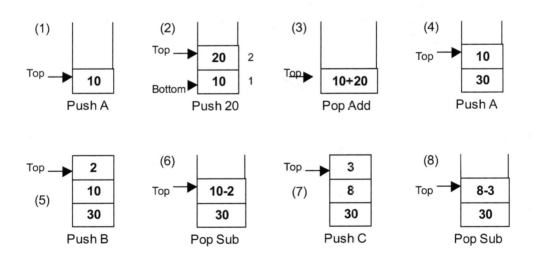

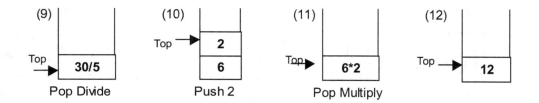

(9)	(10)	(11)	(12)
Top → 30/5	Top → 2, 6	Top → 6*2	Top → 12
Pop Divide	Push 2	Pop Multiply	

How to read and find the values of arithmetic expressions written in Prefix format using the stack.

To find the value of an arithmetic expression in Prefix form using the stack, we use the same method as before, by reading this expression from the right towards the left, and when passing a variable or constant, we push it into the stack using the word Push, and when reading the sign of the calculation, we use the word Pop and then implement it inside the stack, and the following examples show us this.

An example that shows us how to read and evaluate an arithmetic expression in Prefix form. Using the stack, find the result of the arithmetic expression written in the following Infix form:

$$(A * B) + (A - B) / (A-2) \Rightarrow \textbf{Infix}$$

If the value of A=4 and the value of B=2.

Solution: We convert the arithmetic expression from Infix to Prefix using the principle of associating signs with parentheses, and we then get the following formula:

$$+ * AB / -AB - A2 \quad \textbf{Prefix}$$

We read this expression from right to left using push and pop operations and thus get the following operations:

Push 2	This process pushes item 2 into the stack.
Push A	This process pushes element A into the stack
Pop	Perform the calculation
Subtract	Subtraction Process
Push B	This process pushes element B into the stack
Push A	This process pushes element A into the stack
Pop	Perform the calculation
Subtract	Subtraction Process
Pop	Perform the calculation
Divide	Division process
Push B	This process pushes element B into the stack
Push A	This process pushes element A into the stack
Pop	Perform the calculation
Multiply	Multiplication process
Pop	Perform the calculation
Add	Collection process

We represent the arithmetic expression within the stack and substitute directly into the values of the variables, so we get the final result, as shown in the following diagram:

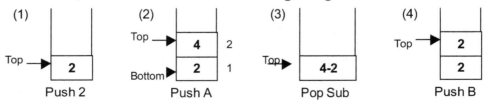

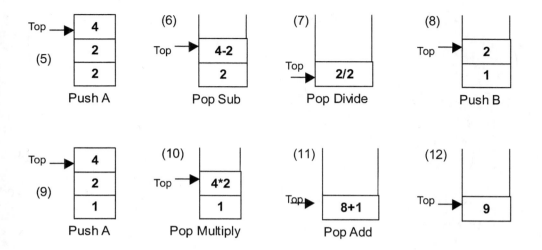

Finally, these are Python software applications on the stack.

You can easily implement stack in Python using built-in lists or using the 'collections.deque' library for better performance. Let's start by explaining how to implement stack using the list:

Use lists to execute Stack

```python
class Stack:
    def __init__(self):
        self.items[] =

    def is_empty(self):
        return len(self.items) == 0

    def push(self, item):
        self.items.append(item)

    def pop(self):
        if not self.is_empty:()
```

```python
            return self.items.pop()
        else:
            raise IndexError("pop from empty stack")

    def peek(self):
        if not self.is_empty:()
            return self.items[1-]
        else:
            raise IndexError("peek from empty stack")

    def size(self):
        return len(self.items)
```

Use 'collections.deque' to execute the Stack 'deque' (short for Double-Ended Queue) from the 'collections' library provides better performance for operations that require adding or removing items from the end of the list.

```python
from collections import deque

class Stack:
    def __init__(self):
        self.items = deque()

    def is_empty(self):
        return len(self.items) == 0

    def push(self, item):
        self.items.append(item)

    def pop(self):
        if not self.is_empty:()
            return self.items.pop()
        else:
            raise IndexError("pop from empty stack")
```

```python
    def peek(self):
        if not self.is_empty:()
            return self.items[1-]
        else:
            raise IndexError("peek from empty stack")

    def size(self):
        return len(self.items)
```

How to use Stack.
Here are some examples of how to use stack:

```python
        stack = Stack()

        # Add elements to the stack

        stack.push(1)
        stack.push(2)
        stack.push(3)

# Check stack size.

print(stack.size())  # Output: 3

# See the item at the top

print(stack.peek())  # Output: 3

 # Remove items from the stack

print(stack.pop())  # Output: 3
print(stack.pop())  # Output: 2

# Check if the stack is empty
print(stack.is_empty())  # Output: False
```

Remove last item

```
print(stack.pop())  # Output: 1
```

Check again if the stack is empty

```
print(stack.is_empty())  # Output: True
```

You have learned how to implement and use stack in Python. Stack can be used in many applications such as managing regressions (such as undoing edits in editors), executing in-depth search algorithms, and others.

Questions on Stacks.

Question 1: Define the stack.

Question 2: What is the difference between a stack and a list?

Question 3: Define the LIFO principle in the stack.

Question 4: Explain the process of adding and dragging with the stack and explain it in the drawing.

Question 5: What are the features of the stack?

Question 6: The number of applications of the stack, and explain one of them.

Question 7: Why is the stack used to call subprograms?

Question 8: If you have a stack with ten integers elements, write a Python program that represents this stack through a connected list.

Question 9: Convert Infix expressions to Postfix and Prefix using the parentheses to signs method

    1. A / B * C + D * E − A * C
    2. (A * B) + (A − B) / (2 * A)
    3. (A / C) + (D * 2)

Question 10: If the value of A=3, B=2, C=5, D=1, read the following arithmetic expressions and calculate the value of each.

    1. AB+C/5+
    2. ABC*/DE*+AC*-
    3. /*+D*/CB3A+AB
    4. /+C2*-+ABC3

❖ Linear Data Structures.
3. Queues.

3.1. Definition of Queue.

A queue is defined as a linear data structure. It is one of the data structures that are used to store data in an organized way that simulates the concept of queue in daily life, where items are added from one side (end of the queue) and items are removed from the other side (the beginning of the queue). The queue can be described by the following concept:

FIFO (First In, First Out): The item that enters first is the one that comes out first. That is, the first operation on the queue is to enter an item, after which the item that entered first can be removed. Queuing is commonly used in various algorithms and applications for its simplicity and efficiency in managing data flow. It is one of the basic tools in many applications, such as task management in operating systems, data processing in networks, and the implementation of various algorithms.

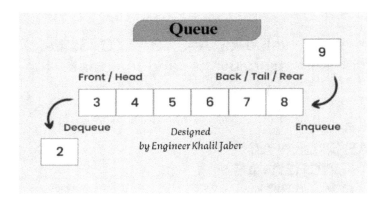

Figure (27) shows the queue

3.2. Basic operations on the queue.
- Enqueue: Add an item to the end of the queue.
- Dequeue: Remove the item from the beginning of the queue.

- Peek/Front (first view in line): Displays the item at the beginning of the queue without removing it.
- IsEmpty: Check if the queue is empty.
- Size: Gets the number of items in the queue.

Illustrative example: Let's say we have an empty queue and want to perform the following operations on it:

- Enqueue 1
- Enqueue 2
- Dequeue
- Enqueue 3
- Peek
- Size

Clarify step-by-step processes:

Enqueue 1	The content of the queue becomes [1]
Enqueue 2	Enter 2 the queue becomes [1, 2]
Dequeue	Item 1 is removed, queue becomes [2]
Enqueue 3	The queue becomes [2, 3]
Peek	The item at the beginning of the queue is 2
Size	The queue size is 2

3.3. Queue types.

Queues are a data structure used to store items in an organized manner, where items are accessed according to certain rules. There are several types of queues, each catering to different needs.

3.3.1 Simple Queue.

3.3.2. Priority queue.

3.3.3. Double Queue or Deque Multiplier.

3.3.4. Circular Queue.

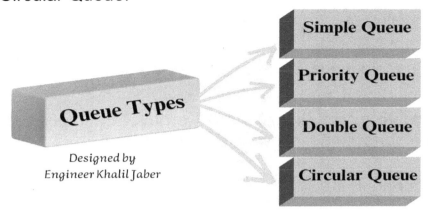

Figure (28) shows the types of queues

Now here's an explanation for each type of queue with an example and code in Python:

3.3.1. Simple Queue.

A regular queue follows the principle of "FIFO: First In, First Out", where items are entered from the end of the queue and removed from the beginning of the queue.

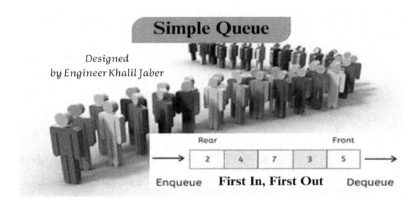

Figure (29) The principle of operation of the simple queue

Example: Imagine a queue in the supermarket where customers are served in the order they arrived.

Python code:

```python
class Queue:
    def __init__(self):
        self.items[] =
    def is_empty(self):
        return len(self.items) == 0
    def enqueue(self, item):
        self.items.append(item)

    def dequeue(self):
        if self.is_empty:()
            return None
        return self.items.pop(0)
    def peek(self):
        if self.is_empty:()
            return None
        return self.items[0]
    def size(self):
        return len(self.items)
```

 # Example of use

```python
q = Queue()
q.enqueue(1)
q.enqueue(2)
q.enqueue(3)
print(q.dequeue())  # Output: 1
print(q.peek())     # Output: 2
print(q.size())     # Output: 2
```

3.3.2. Priority Queue.

A priority queue is similar to a regular queue, but each item has a priority that determines when it is removed from the queue. The item with the highest priority is output first.

Example: Imagine an emergency room in a hospital where patients are treated based on the severity of their condition.

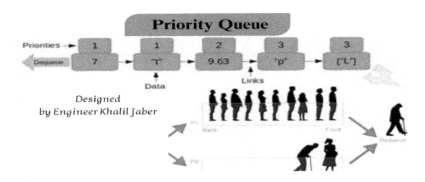

Figure (30) The principle of operation of the priority queue

Python code:

```python
import heapq
class PriorityQueue:
    def __init__(self):
        self.heap[] =

    def is_empty(self):
        return len(self.heap) == 0

    def enqueue(self, item, priority):
        heapq.heappush(self.heap, (priority, item))

    def dequeue(self):
        if self.is_empty:()
            return None
        return heapq.heappop(self.heap)[1]

    def peek(self):
        if self.is_empty:()
            return None
```

```
        return self.heap[0[1][

    def size(self):
        return len(self.heap)
```

Example of use.

```
pq = PriorityQueue()
pq.enqueue("patient1", 3)
pq.enqueue("patient2", 1)
pq.enqueue("patient3", 2)
print(pq.dequeue())  # Output: patient2(Highest priority)
print(pq.peek())     # Output: patient3
print(pq.size())     # Output: 2
```

3.3.3. Deque Double-Ended Queue.

The double queue allows insertion and removal from both ends, and can be considered a combination of a regular queue and a stack.
Example: Imagine a queue in a movie queue where people can enter from the front or from the back.

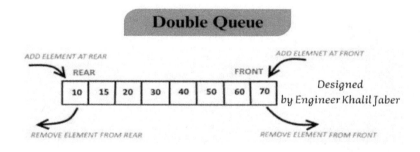

Figure (31) The principle of double queue

Python code:

105

```python
from collections import deque
class Deque:
    def __init__(self):
        self.deque = deque()

    def is_empty(self):
        return len(self.deque) == 0

    def add_front(self, item):
        self.deque.appendleft(item)

    def add_rear(self, item):
        self.deque.append(item)

    def remove_front(self):
        if self.is_empty:()
            return None
        return self.deque.popleft()

    def remove_rear(self):
        if self.is_empty:()
            return None
        return self.deque.pop()

    def peek_front(self):
        if self.is_empty:()
            return None
        return self.deque[0]

    def peek_rear(self):
        if self.is_empty:()
            return None
        return self.deque[1-]

    def size(self):
        return len(self.deque)
```

Example of use.

```
dq = Deque()
dq.add_rear(1)
dq.add_rear(2)
dq.add_front(0)
print(dq.remove_front()) # Output: 0
print(dq.remove_rear())  # Output: 2
print(dq.peek_front())   # Output: 1
print(dq.size())         # Output: 1
```

3.3.4. Circular Queue.

A circular queue is a type of queue where the back end is connected to the beginning of the queue, allowing efficient use of available space.

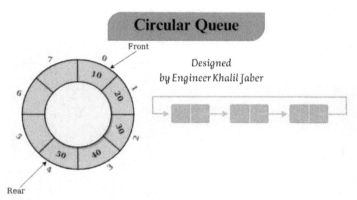

Figure (32) The principle of circular queue

Example: Imagine a queue in a game of musical chairs where the cycle continues non-stop.

Python code:

```
class CircularQueue:
```

```python
def __init__(self, max_size):
    self.queue = [None] * max_size
    self.max_size = max_size
    self.front = -1
    self.rear = -1

def is_empty(self):
    return self.front == -1

def is_full(self):
    return (self.rear + 1) % self.max_size == self.front

def enqueue(self, item):
    if self.is_full:()
        return "Queue is full"
    if self.is_empty:()
        self.front = 0
    self.rear = (self.rear + 1) % self.max_size
    self.queue[self.rear] = item

def dequeue(self):
    if self.is_empty:()
        return None
    item = self.queue[self.front]
    if self.front == self.rear:
        self.front = -1
        self.rear = -1
    else:
        self.front = (self.front + 1) % self.max_size
    return item

def peek(self):
    if self.is_empty:()
        return None
    return self.queue[self.front]
```

```python
    def size(self):
        if self.is_empty:()
            return 0
        if self.rear >= self.front:
            return self.rear - self.front + 1
        return self.max_size - self.front + self.rear + 1
```

Example of use.
```python
cq = CircularQueue(3)
cq.enqueue(1)
cq.enqueue(2)
cq.enqueue(3)
print(cq.enqueue(4))  # Output: Queue is full
print(cq.dequeue())   # Output: 1
print(cq.enqueue(4))  # Works now as space is available
print(cq.peek())      # Output: 2
print(cq.size())      # Output: 3
```

❖ **Linear Data Structures.**
4. Queue Dic.

4.1. Definition of Queue Dic.

Queue Dic. It is the abbreviation of "Double-Ended Queue", a data structure that allows adding and deleting items from both ends, i.e. from the front and back, unlike the regular queue, which only allows adding from the back and deleting from the front. (See figure 31 above).

4.2. Characteristics of Queue Dic.

- Add from both ends: Items can be added at the beginning or end of the queue.
- Delete from both ends: Items can be removed from the beginning or end of the queue.
- Dynamic: The size of a queue Dic. can change dynamically with the addition and removal of items.

4.3. Basic Operations of Queue Dic.

- Add in front (addFirst/push_front): Adds an item at the beginning of the queue.
- Add at the back (addLast / push_back): Adds an item at the end of the queue.
- Delete from front (removeFirst/pop_front): Removes an item from the beginning of the queue.
- Delete from back (removeLast / pop_back): Removes an item from the end of the queue.
- Search for items: You can search for specific items, and the first and last item can be accessed without removing them.

4.4. Uses of Queue Dic.

- Memory management: where the queue is used to store items that need to be processed at both ends.
- Algorithms: Used in some algorithms where there is a need to access items from both ends quickly.

- Interactive systems: Used in applications that require smooth handling of incoming and outgoing data.

4.5. Compare queue with other data structures.

- Queue: Allows adding from the back and deleting from the front only.
- Stack: Allows addition and deletion from one side only (top).
- Disjointed queue: More flexible than regular queue and stack, as operations are allowed from both ends.

Example:

Figure (33) Queue Dic.

In the diagram above, you can see a representation of the deque. Items are arranged from left to right, with "Front" and "Back" tags to indicate where items can be added or removed. In this example, the items in the disjointed queue are ['b', 'a', 'c']:

- A new element can be added in the foreground after 'b'.
- A new element can be added at the back after 'c'.
- The 'b' can be removed from the front or 'c' from the back.

This shows how a disassembled queue can handle operations from both ends flexibly.

Programming example (using Python)

```
from collections import deque
```

```
# Create a disjointed queue

dq = deque()
```

 # Add items

```
dq.append('a')      # Add on the back
dq.appendleft('b')   # Add in front

# Remove items
dq.pop ()      # Remove from back
dq.popleft ()    # Remove from front
```

 # View queue

```
    print(dq)
```

Note: The basic operations of a disjointed queue (adding and deleting from both ends) are usually fast and take place in a fixed time (O(1), making it very effective in applications that need quick access from both ends. Overall, a disjointed queue is a robust and flexible data structure used in many applications that require dynamic and fast processing of items from both ends.

❖ **Linear Data Structures.**
5.   Set (Group).

5.1.   Definition of Set (Group).

Sets are a type of data structure that allows items to be stored so that they are unique and unordered. Groups support a range of operations such as adding and deleting items, checking for an item, and operations between our groups such as union, intersection, and teams.

A set is a mathematical model of a set of different objects, a set contains elements or members, which can be mathematical objects of any kind, numbers, symbols, points in space, lines, other geometric shapes, variables, or even other groups. To better understand sets, let's take, for example, the Venn diagram as follows:

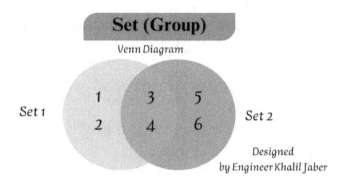

Figure (34) Basic operations on collections in a Venn diagram.

In the diagram above, we can see the Venn Diagram representing Basic operations on groups 'Set 1' and 'Set 2'.

- The left area (green part) represents the unique elements of 'Set 1', which is {1, 2}.
- The right area (blue part) represents the unique elements of 'Set 2', which is {5, 6}.
- Common area (intersection): Represents the common elements between 'Set 1' and 'Set 2', which are {3, 4}.

This drawing helps to visually understand the relationships between groups and makes operations on groups easier to understand.

5.2. Operations on groups represented in the diagram.

- Union: All elements in both groups: {1, 2, 3, 4, 5, 6}.
- Intersection: Elements common to the two groups: {3, 4}.
- Difference:
- Difference between 'Set 1' and 'Set 2': Items in 'Set 1' that are not in 'Set 2', which is {1, 2}.
- Difference between 'Set 2' and 'Set 1': Items in 'Set 2' and not in 'Set 1', which is {5, 6}.
- Symmetric Difference: Elements in one group and not in the other, which are {1, 2, 5, 6}.

5.3. Characteristics of groups.

- Non-Duplication: Groups do not allow duplicate items. Each item in the collection is unique.
- Disorder: The items in the group are unordered. Items cannot be accessed via a specific index.
- Efficiency of operations: Basic operations such as adding, deleting, and checking for the presence of an item are done in almost constant time ($O(1)$).

5.4. Basic operations on groups.

- Add Item (Add): Adds a new item to the collection.
- Delete an item (remove) to remove a specific item from the collection. If the item does not exist, it raises an error.
- Delete an item without error (discard) to remove a specific item from the collection without raising an error if the item does not exist.
- Check for an item (in) to check if the item exists in the group.

- Remove All Items (clear) to remove all items from the collection.
- Copy the group (copy) to create a copy of the collection.

5.5. Operations on groups mathematically.

- Union creates a group that contains all elements from two groups.
- Intersection Creates a collection that contains the elements shared by two groups.
- Difference creates a group that contains items that are in one group and not in the other.
- Symmetric difference (symmetric_difference) Creates a group that contains items that are in one group and not in the other.

Example: Programmatic using Python.

Create two groups.

```
set1 = {1, 2, 3, 4}
set2 = {3, 4, 5, 6}
```

Add items.

```
set1.add(7)
set2.add(8)
```

Delete items

```
set1.remove(7)
```

Does not raise an error if the item does not exist.

```
set2.discard(8)
```

Check for an item.

```python
print(2 in set1)  # True
print(8 in set2)  # False
```

Operations on groups.

```python
union_set = set1.union(set2)
intersection_set = set1.intersection(set2)
difference_set = set1.difference(set2)
symmetric_difference_set =
set1.symmetric_difference(set2)
```

Print results.

```python
print("Set 1:", set1)
print("Set 2:", set2)
print("Union:", union_set)
print("Intersection:", intersection_set)
print("Difference (Set1 - Set2):", difference_set)
print("Symmetric Difference:", symmetric_difference_set)
```

Detailed explanation of the code.

1. Create two groups.

```python
set1 = {1, 2, 3, 4}
set2 = {3, 4, 5, 6}
```

Here, two groups 'set1' and 'set2' are created with some numbers.

2. Add items.

```python
Set1.add(7)
```

```
Set2.add(8)
```

Element '7' is added to 'set1' and element '8' to 'set2'.

3. Delete items.

```
Set1.remove(7)
Set2.discard(8)
```

Element '7' is removed from 'set1' using 'remove', and element '8' is removed from 'set2' using 'discard', which does not raise an error if the element does not exist.

4. Check for an item.

```
print(2 in set1)  # True
print(8 in set2)  # False
```

Element '2' is checked in 'set1' and element '8' in 'set2'.

5. Operations on groups.

```
union_set = set1.union(set2)
intersection_set = set1.intersection(set2)
difference_set = set1.difference(set2)
symmetric_difference_set =
set1.symmetric_difference(set2)
```

- 'union' creates a collection containing all the elements from 'set1' and 'set2'.
- 'intersection' creates a collection containing the elements shared between 'set1' and 'set2'.
- 'difference' creates a collection that contains the elements in 'set1' and not in 'set2'.

- 'symmetric_difference' creates a group that contains items that are in one group and not in the other.

6. Print the results.

```
print("Set 1:", set1)
print("Set 2:", set2)
print("Union:", union_set)
print("Intersection:", intersection_set)
print("Difference (Set1 - Set2):", difference_set)
print("Symmetric Difference:",
symmetric_difference_set)
```

The contents of the groups and the results resulting from operations are printed in the collections. With this detailed explanation, it is possible to understand how groups work in data structures and use them in a programming language Python.

| ❖ Linear Data Structures. |
| 6. Strings. |

6.1. Definition of String.

A string is generally a type of data and is usually represented as superstrings of bytes (or words) that store a string of characters. It is defined as a set of characters. The difference between a character array and a string is that the string ends with a special character '0'. A string is a sequence of letters that can include alphabets, numbers, symbols and spaces.

It is a type of data that represents a string of characters. They are used for storing and processing texts. There are several types of strings, which differ in how they are stored and processed, but the basic concept is that they consist of a set of characters (symbols).

String str=" Jaber"

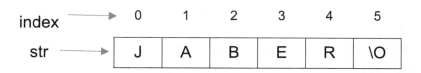

index	0	1	2	3	4	5
str	J	A	B	E	R	\O

Figure (35) shows the series.

6.2. The importance of String.

In most programming languages, text strings are treated as a distinct data type. This means that string have their own set of operations and properties. They can be advertised and processed using specific string-related functions and methods.

-   Strings are an essential part of programming because they represent the primary way of dealing with text.
-   Strings are used in input and output operations (such as reading from files or displaying text on the screen).
-   Strings play an important role in data processing, searching, and sorting information.

In short, strings are one of the most widely used and important data structures in programming, making understanding them and how to handle them essential for programmers. Here are some basic concepts related to staring.

- Length: Indicates the number of characters in the string.
- Indexing: Any character in a string can be accessed by indexing, and indexing usually starts from scratch.
- Storage: Strings can be stored in memory in different ways depending on the programming language, but they are often stored as arrays of characters.

6.3. Common operations on String.

- Concatenation: Combine two strings together to form a new one. For example, merging the BIRD string with the DOG string gives the BIRDDOG string.
- Slicing: Extracting part of the string. Where the substring is determined by specifying the first location and the last location in the string, for example, the 4-7 position in the string is tail of two cities, substring e of.
- Pattern matching: Find a specific position or part within a string. That is, the search is for the repetition of a string in another string, for example, the baseball string is repeated in the modern baseball string, starting from the 8th position.
  - Substitution: Replacing part of the string with another part.
  - Deletion where the symbol or substring to be deleted from the original string is determined by knowing the first location of the substring to be deleted.
  - Conversion: Converts a string to another format, such as converting letters to uppercase or lowercase.

Example in the Python programming language.

```
text = "Hello, World"!
print(text[0])   # H
print(text[7:12]) # World
```

```
print(len(text))  # 13
new_text = text + " How are you"?
print(new_text)   # Hello, World! How are you?
```

6.4. Storage of Strings.

Strings can be stored in memory in different ways depending on the programming language, but they are often stored as arrays of characters. They are stored in one of the following ways:

6.4.1. The method of fixed-length strings.

In this method, each string is reserved a specific number of sites in memory and the string codes are stored in these sites, and in the case of surplus sites, they are stored in space and cannot be used by another string, and these spaces are considered one of the disadvantages of this method, as it leads to wasting memory and not being well exploited.

6.4.2. Index Table Workspace Method.

In this method, the starting tables are built in which the beginning of each string is determined, and the length table is constructed, in each entry in which the length of each string is determined in the area vector.

6.4.3. Linked lists method.

Strings are represented in this way by binary circular lists, where each letter of the string is represented in a node with two pointers, a front pointer and a back pointer.

6.5. Types of Strings.

There are several types of text strings in data structures, and these types vary depending on the context and the programming language used. Here are five common types:

6.5.1. Fixed Strings.

These strings cannot be modified after they are created. Any change requires the creation of a new string.
Example: In Python, text strings are immutable.

```
text = "Hello"
text = "Hello, World "!  # A new string is created.
```

6.5.2. Mutable Strings.

These strings can be modified after they are created without having to create a new one.

6.5.3. Empty Strings.

A string containing zero characters. They are useful for representing blank texts.

Example:
```
empty_string"" =
print(len(empty_string))  # 0
```

6.5.4. Multi-line Strings.

Text strings that span multiple lines. They are useful when writing long texts or texts that contain new lines.

Example: Three quotation marks can be used to create multi-line strings.

```
multiline_string = """This is a string
```

```
that spans multiple
lines""".
print(multiline_string)
```

6.5.5. Raw Strings.

Used to represent strings without having to escape special characters (such as backslash).

Example: The letter 'r' can be used before the string.

```
raw_string = r"C:\Users\Name\Documents"
print(raw_string)  # C:\Users\Name\Documents
```

These types help to deal with texts in different ways depending on the special requirements of the project or program. Understanding how to use each type can contribute to writing more effective and efficient programs.

6.4.A. Fixed Length Strings.

They are data structures or data types used in programming where the length of a string is predetermined and remains constant throughout its use. These strings can be useful in certain cases where it is necessary to know the maximum size of data in advance or when performance is important. Here is a detailed explanation of these strings:

- **The main characteristics of fixed-length strings:**

1. Its length is pre-fixed: The length of the string is determined when it is created and cannot be changed later.
2. Memory management: Since the size is known in advance, the memory can be allocated accurately without having to reallocate it.

3. Efficiency: Operations on fixed-length strings are often faster because they do not require dynamic length calculations or memory reassignment.

- **Advantages:**

1. Improved performance: Because the size is fixed, operations on the string are faster and do not require memory reassignment.
2. Easy memory management: Knowing the size in advance helps in accurately allocating memory.
3. Reduce errors: Avoid errors resulting from exceeding limits where the length is fixed and known.
- **Defects**:

1. Lack of flexibility: The length cannot be changed after it is defined, which makes fixed-length strings less flexible compared to dynamic strings.
2. Memory Wasp: If the specified length is greater than required, memory may be wasted.
3. Complexity of content management: Handling frequently changing content can be more complex compared to dynamic string.

- **Common Uses:**

1. Embedded systems: where resources are limited and known in advance.
2. Network protocols: where stacks are of fixed size.
3. Real-time applications: where it is necessary to obtain consistent and expected performance.

Fixed-length strings are a good choice in applications that require strict memory management and high performance, but they may be inappropriate in cases where greater flexibility is needed in handling variable data.

How to use it in Python: Using a list to simulate a fixed-length string In Python, a list can be used to simulate a fixed-length string as follows:

```python
class FixedLengthString:
    def __init__(self, length):
        self.length = length
# Initialize the list with blank characters
        self.data = [' '] * length

    def set_string(self, input_string):
        if len(input_string) > self.length:
            raise ValueError("Input string exceeds fixed length")
        for i in range(self.length):
            if i < len(input_string):
                self.data[i] = input_string[i]
            else:
# Fill in the blanks if the length is less
                self.data[i]  ' ' =
    def get_string(self):
        return ''.join(self.data)

    def __str__(self):
        return self.get_string()
```

How to use:

```python
fixed_str = FixedLengthString(10)
fixed_str.set_string("Hello")
print(fixed_str) #  output' :Hello'
fixed_str.set_string("Pythonistas")
```

This will raise an exception due to exceeding the specified length. Using the method described above, fixed-length strings can be simulated in Python, providing some performance benefits and memory management in certain applications.

6.4.B. Indexed Strings.

They are text strings whose individual elements can be accessed using indexes. Strings in Python are immutable, which means that a string cannot be modified after it is created, but new strings can be created based on certain modifications. Here is an explanation of how to handle indexed strings in Python:

- Access string elements: Any character in the text string can be accessed using its index in square brackets '[]'. Remember that the index starts from zero.

    ```
    s = "Hello, World"!
    print(s[0])  # H
    print(s[7])  # W
    ```

- Reverse indexing: Passive indexing can be used to access characters from the end. Index '-1' indicates the last character in the string.

    ```
    print(s[-1])! #
    print(s[-2])  # d
    ```

- Slicing: You can extract part of the text string using Slicing. The beginning and end of the part to be cut are determined with the possibility of determining the cutting step.

    ```
    print(s[0:5])   # Hello
    ```

```
print(s[7:12])  # World
print(s[::2])   # Hlo ol!
```

- Modify the text string: Since text strings are not changeable, any modification to them means creating a new text string. Shredder and parts can be used.

```
s = "Hello, World"!
new_s = s[:7] + "Universe"!
print(new_s) # Hello, Universe!
```

- Some useful functions for text strings: There are many useful functions that can be used with text strings:

  ➢ **len()**: To get the length of the text string.
  ➢ **upper()**:To uppercase all characters.
  ➢ **lower ()**: Converts all characters to lowercase.
  ➢ **find()**: to search for part of the text string.
  ➢ **replace ()**:To replace part of a text string with another.

```
s = "Hello, World"!
print(len(s))       # 13
print(s.upper())    # HELLO, WORLD!
print(s.lower())    # hello, world!
print(s.find("World")) # 7
print(s.replace("World", "Universe"))# Hello, Universe!
```

- Duplicate text strings: The text string can be repeated using the multiplication operator '*'.

```
s = "Hi" !
print(s * 3) # Hi! Hi! Hi !
```

− Check for a part in the text string: The 'in' operator can be used to check if part of the string exists within another string.

```
s = "Hello, World"!
print("World" in s)  # True
print("Universe" in s)  # False
```

These are some of the basics for working with indexed strings in Python. Text strings are powerful and flexible, and provide many tools to make it easier to work with text.

6.4.C. Linked List Strings.

Representing strings using lists means converting a string of characters to a list where each item in the list is a character from the original string. We can also use lists to directly represent strings of characters.

− Convert string to list: To convert a string to a list of characters, the list function can be used in Python.

Original String.

```
string = "Hello, World"!
```

Convert string to list.

```
char_list = list(string)
print(char_list)
```

The result will be:

```
['!' ,'H', 'e', 'l', 'l', 'o', ',', ' ', 'W', 'o', 'r', 'l', 'd']
```

- Create a list to represent a string: We can also create a list to represent a specific string by specifying characters directly within the lists. Case in point:

    # Create a list to represent a string.

    char_list = ['H', 'e', 'l', 'l', 'o']

    # Convert list to string with join function.
    string = ''.join(char_list)
    print(string)

    # The result will be: Hello

- Working with lists as strings: We can use lists to represent strings and manipulate them in different ways.

For example, we can modify the characters in the string through the List:

    # Create a list to represent a string.

    char_list = ['H', 'e', 'l', 'l', 'o']

    # Edit a character in the list.

    char_list[0] = 'J'

    # Convert list to new string.

    new_string = ''.join(char_list)
    print(new_string)

    # The result will be: Jello

- Additional examples: Reverse a string using lists. Where we can reverse a string using lists as follows:

```
# Original Sring.
string = "Hello, World"!

# Convert string to list.
char_list = list(string)

# Reverse the list.
char_list.reverse()

# Convert flipped list to string.
reversed_string = ''.join(char_list)
print(reversed_string)

# The result will be:
!dlroW ,olleH
```

- Check for a character in the string: We can check for a character in the string using the lists:

```
# Original Series.
string = "Hello, World"!

# Convert string to list.
char_list = list(string)

# Check for a specific character.
if 'H' in char_list:
print("The character 'H' is in the string.")
else:
print("The character 'H' is not in the string.")

# The result will be:
```

❑ Linear Data Structures.
7. Alphabet.

7.1. Definition of Alphabet.

Alphabets in data structures are a set of symbols (or letters) that are used to create words or text strings in various applications. Alphabets are used in many fields such as word processing, coding, and algorithm design. Alphabets can be divided into different types based on their use and context.

7.2. Types of Alphabets.

- Binary Alphabet: consists of only two letters: '0' and '1'.
- It is widely used in digital computing and data processing.
- Decimal Alphabet: consists of 10 numbers: '0', '1', '2', '3', '4', '5', '6', '7', '8', '9'. They are used in everyday calculations.
- The English alphabet consists of 26 letters: 'A' to 'Z'. It is used in English languages and most programming languages.
- The hexadecimal alphabet consists of 16 symbols: '0' to '9' and 'A' to 'F'. They are used in digital encryption and memory address.

Programming examples using Python We will write an example that shows how to deal with different alphabets in Python.

Binary alphabet.
```
    binary_alphabet['1' ,'0'] =
    print("Binary Alphabet:", binary_alphabet)
```

Decimal alphabet.
```
    decimal_alphabet = [str(i) for i in range(10)]
    print("Decimal Alphabet:", decimal_alphabet)
```

English alphabet.
```
    english_alphabet = [chr(i) for i in range(65, 91)]
    print("English Alphabet:", english_alphabet)
```

Hex alphabet.
```
    hexadecimal_alphabet = [str(i) for i in range(10)] + [chr(i)
    for i in range(65, 71)]
    print("Hexadecimal Alphabet:", hexadecimal_alphabet)
```

Practical application: Let's write code that converts a decimal number to a representation in the hexadecimal alphabet.

```
    def decimal_to_hexadecimal(decimal_number):
       if decimal_number == 0:
          return "0"

    hexadecimal_alphabet = [str(i) for i in range(10)] + [chr(i) for i
in range(65, 71)]
    hexadecimal"" =

    while decimal_number > 0:
       remainder = decimal_number % 16
       hexadecimal = hexadecimal_alphabet[remainder] +
hexadecimal
       decimal_number //= 16
```

7.3. The difference between strings and alphabets.

In data structures, there is a difference between the concept of alphabets and string. Let's separate the differences between them:

- **Alphabets:**
- Definition: Alphabets are a specific set of symbols or letters that can be used to build words or strings.

Example: The English alphabet consists of 26 letters (A-Z). It can also include special numbers or symbols depending on the system used.

- Use in data structures: Alphabets are used to determine the possible set of symbols that strings can consist of.

For **example**, in text encryption or in defining patterns in text search algorithms.

- **String:**
- Definition: A string is a sequence of characters that is grouped together to form text or a word.

Example: "Hello, World!" or "12345".

- Use in data structures: Strings are used to store and process texts. It can include operations on strings such as find, replace, hash, and merge.

❏ **Main differences:**
- Concept: An alphabet is a set of possible characters, while a string is a certain sequence of characters.
- Usage: Alphabets are used to define the range of possible characters, while strings are used to represent and store text.

- Definition: The alphabet is static and predefined (e.g. language characters), while strings are dynamic and can change (e.g. user texts).
- Processing: Alphabetical processing is usually about determining the range of letters or symbols, while string processing is about dealing with actual texts such as editing and searching.

In other words, alphabets are the "base blocks" that are used to build strings, while strings are the entities we actually work on when dealing with text in data structures. This has covered the concept of alphabets in data structures and reviewed some basic types with programming examples and illustrations.

8.1. Definition of Files.

Files are one of the primaries means of storing data permanently. Files are used to store data so that it can be accessed later, even after you close the program. Files can contain text, images, videos, or any other type of data. In the context of data structures, files are used to represent and store data structures such as lists, dictionaries, trees, etc.

8.2. Files Types.

8.2.1. Text Files: Used to store text data. Each character in the file is stored as text.
8.2.2. Binary Files: Used to store data in binary format, which is useful for storing complex data or large files.

8.3. Methods to work with Files in Python.

❏ Open and close files: To use files in Python, you can use the Open and Close functions

Open File.
```
file = open('example.txt', 'r')  # 'r 'To read
```

Read the content of the file
```
content = file.read()
```

Close file
```
file.close()
```

❏ Read and write files: You can read and write data from files using several methods, such as 'read', 'readline', 'readlines' to read, 'write' and 'writelines' to write.

Read the whole file content.
```
    with open('example.txt', 'r') as file:
        content = file.read()
```

Write text to file.
```
    with open('example.txt', 'w') as file:
        file.write('Hello, World!')
```

8.4.   Working with Binary Files.

Write binary data to file.
```
    with open('example.bin', 'wb') as file:
        file.write(b'\x00\x01\x02\x03')
```

Read binary data from file.
```
    with open('example.bin', 'rb') as file:
        data = file.read()
```

Examples of practical applications.

❏ Store data in a list: A list is written to a text file as follows:
```
data= [1,2,3,4,5]
    with open('data.txt', 'w') as file:
        for item in data:
            file.write(f"{item}\n")
```

Read data from text file to list.
```
    with open('data.txt', 'r') as file:
        data = [int(line.strip()) for line in file]
    print(data)    # [1,2,3,4,5]
```

❏ Store data in a dictionary.

```python
import json

# Write dictionary to text file using JSON.
data = {'name': 'Alice', 'age': 25}
with open('data.json', 'w') as file:
    json.dump(data, file)

# Read data from text file to dictionary.
with open('data.json', 'r') as file:
    data = json.load(file)
print(data)  # {'name': 'Alice', 'age': 25}
```

❑ Store data in a complex data structure (such as a tree)

```python
import pickle

# Simple tree definition.
class Node:
    def __init__(self, value):
        self.value = value
        self.left = None
        self.right = None
root = Node(10)
root.left = Node(5)
root.right = Node(15)

# Write the tree to a binary file using pickle.
with open('tree.pkl', 'wb') as file:
    pickle.dump(root, file)

# Read the tree from a binary file.
with open('tree.pkl', 'rb') as file:
    root = pickle.load(file)
print(root.value)  # 10
print(root.left.value)  # 5
print(root.right.value)  # 15
```

Conclusion: Files are an important part of permanent data management in programming applications. With Python, you can easily open, read, and write text and binary files, making it easier for you to store and retrieve data structures when needed. Of course, here I will explain more details and examples of how to handle files in Python and how to use files to store various data structures.

Open and close files: To open a file in Python, we use the Open function. Files can be opened in different modes such as read ("r"), write ("w"), add ("a"), and read and write binary ("rb", "wb"). After you open the file, you must close it with close to ensure that resources are released correctly. However, the problems of forgetting to close the file can be avoided by using the context 'with' which automatically closes the file after it is finished.

Open and read the file with 'with' in Python.
```
    with open('example.txt', 'r') as file:
        content = file.read()
        print(content)
```

No need to use file.close() when using 'with'
Read files.
- Read the entire file.
```
    with open('example.txt', 'r') as file:
        content = file.read()
        print(content)
```

- Read the file line by line.
```
    with open('example.txt', 'r') as file:
        for line in file:
    print(line.strip())
    #Remove excess whitespace
    strip().
```

Use of 'Redlin()' and 'Redlins()'

```
with open('example.txt', 'r') as file:
line = file.readline() # Read one line
print(line)
# Read all lines and return them as a list
lines = file.readlines()
print(lines)
```

Write to file: When the file is opened in write mode ("w"), the old content of the file is deleted.

```
with open('example.txt', 'w') as file:
file.write('Hello, World!\n')
file.write('This is a new line.\n')
```

Add to file: When you open the file in Add mode ("a"), add to the end of the file without deleting the old content.

```
with open('example.txt', 'a') as file:
file.write('Appending a new line.\n')
```

8.5. Dealing with binary Files.

Write and read binary data: You can use binary mode to write and read data that is not text, such as images or executables.

Write binary data.

```
with open('example.bin', 'wb') as file:
file.write(b'\x00\x01\x02\x03')
```

Read binary data.

```
with open('example.bin', 'rb') as file:
data = file.read()
print(data)
```

Storing data structures in files.
Storing lists.

Write list to text file.
```python
Data= [1,2,3,4,5]
with open('data.txt', 'w') as file:
    for item in data:
        file.write(f"{item}\n")
```

Read a list from a text file.
```python
with open('data.txt', 'r') as file:
data = [int(line.strip()) for line in file]
print(data)
```

Store dictionaries using JSON.
```python
import json
```

Write dictionary to text file.
```python
data = {'name': 'Alice', 'age': 25}
with open('data.json', 'w') as file:
 json.dump(data, file)
```

Read a dictionary from a text file.
```python
with open('data.json', 'r') as file:
data = json.load(file)
print(data)
```

Store complex data structures using pickle.
```python
import pickle
```

Simple tree definition.
```python
class Node:
    def __init__(self, value):
        self.value = value
        self.left = None
        self.right = None
root = Node(10)
root.left = Node(5)
root.right = Node(15)
```

Write the tree to a binary file.

```
with open('tree.pkl', 'wb') as file:
    pickle.dump(root, file)
```

Read the tree from a binary file.

```
with open('tree.pkl', 'rb') as file:
root = pickle.load(file)
print(root.value)  # 10
print(root.left.value)  # 5
print(root.right.value)  # 15
```

Good practices when dealing with files.

- Use 'with': Always use the context 'with' to open files to ensure they close properly even if exceptions occur.
- Handle exceptions: Use the 'try' and 'except' blocks to handle possible errors while working with files.
- Check for file existence: Check for the existence of the file before trying to read or write to it using 'os.path.exists'.

```
import os
if os.path.exists('example.txt'):
    with open('example.txt', 'r') as file:
        content = file.read()
        print(content)
else:
    print("File does not exist.")
```

❑ **Conclusion**: Handling files in Python is an essential part of many applications. Files can permanently store text, binary, and complex data structures, allowing them to be retrieved and processed later. With the right tools like 'json' and 'pickle', you can easily store and retrieve structured data and complex data structures.

End of Chapter 2

# Chapter 3:

❑ **Variable data structures (Nonlinear structures).**

1. **Trees.**
2. **Graph.**

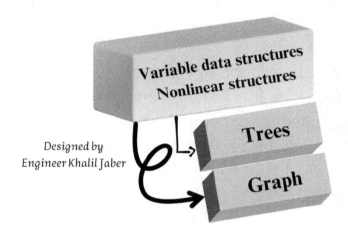

1.1. Definition of trees:

Trees are one of the most important and used data structures in computer science. The structure of the tree consists of a group of Nodes linked to each other in a hierarchical manner so that there is a single path between any two nodes of the tree and in general the tree consists of the following:

- Root: It is the upper node in the tree.
- Nodes: Represents the points in the tree.
- Edges: The links that connect the nodes to each other.
- Leaves: Contracts that do not have children.
-

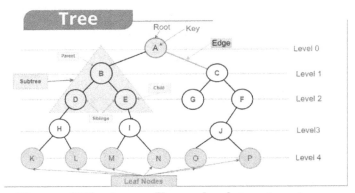

Figure (36) shows Trees in data structures.

1.2. Characteristics of Trees:

The trees in the data structures are characterized by the following:

- Number of edges: An edge can be defined as the connection between two nodes. If the tree has N nodes, it will have edges (N-1).
- Node depth: Node depth is defined as the length of the path from root to that node. Each edge adds one length unit to the path. So, it can also be defined as the number of edges in the path from the root of the tree to the node.
- Node height: Node height can be defined as the length of the longest path from the node to the leaf node of the tree.
- Tree height: Tree height is the length of the longest path from the root of the tree to the node of the leaf of the tree.
- Node Score: The total number of subtrees associated with that node is called the node score. The tree grade is the maximum node score between all the nodes in the tree.

1.3. What is the structure of tree data?

A tree data structure is a hierarchical structure used to represent and organize data in a way that is easy to navigate and search. It is a set of nodes bound by edges and has a hierarchical relationship between nodes.

The top node in the tree is called the root, and the nodes below it is called the child nodes. Each node can have multiple child nodes, and these child nodes can also have their own child nodes, forming a redundant structure.

1.4. Terms in the tree data structure.

- Parent node: A node that is a precursor to a node is called the parent node of that node. For example, if we look at Figure 36, we will find that {B} is the original node of {D, E}.

- Sub node: The node that is the immediate successor to the node is called the child node of that node. For example, from the previous figure 36, {D, E} are the sub nodes of {B}.
- Root node: The upper node of a tree or node that does not contain any parent node is called the root node. For example, from Figure 36 above, {A} is the root node of the tree. A non-empty tree should have exactly one root node and exactly one path from the root to all other nodes in the tree.
- Leaf node or outer node: Nodes that do not have any sub nodes are called paper nodes. For example, in Figure 36 above, the knots {K, L, M, N, O, P} are the leaf nodes of the tree.
- Node Ancestor: Any previous nodes on the root path to that node are called the ancestors of that node. As shown in the previous Figure 36 {A, B} are the original nodes of node {E}.
- Scion: Node X is a descendant of another node Y if and only if Y is the ancestor of Y.
- Siblings: Children from the same parent node are called brothers. {D, E} They are called siblings.
- Node level: The number of path edges from the root node to that node. The root node has level 0.
- Inner node: A node that contains at least one branch is called an inner node.
- Node neighbor: The parent or child nodes of that node are called neighbors of that node.
- Subtree: Any node of a tree with its descendant.

1.5. The advantages of the tree.
- The tree provides effective search depending on the tree type, with average search times O (log n) for balanced trees such as AVL.

- Trees provide a hierarchical representation of data, making it easy to organize and navigate large amounts of information.
- The vertical nature of trees makes it easy to traverse and process them using vertical algorithms.

1.6. Disadvantages of the tree.

- Unbalanced trees, which means that the height of the tree is tilted towards one side, which can lead to inefficient search times.
- Trees require more memory space requirements than some other data structures such as arrays and linked lists, especially if the tree is very large.
- Implementing and processing trees can be complex and require a good understanding of algorithms.

1.7. Apply tree data structure:

- File System: This enables efficient navigation and organization of files.
- Data compression: Hoffman markup is a common method of data compression that involves creating a binary tree where sheets represent characters and how often they occur. The resulting tree is used to encode the data in such a way as to reduce the required storage size.
- Compiler design: In compiler design, a syntax tree is used to represent the structure of the program.
- Database indexing: B trees and other tree structures are used to index the database to search and retrieve data efficiently.

1.8. Tree Types:
1.8.1 Binary tree:

It is a non-linear tree in which each node has at most two branches. It has a hierarchical structure in which its two branches are referred to as the left child and the right child. They are commonly used in computer science to store and retrieve data efficiently, with various operations such as insertion, deletion, and traversal.

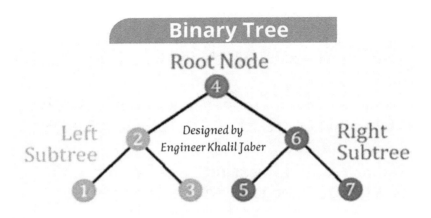

Figure (37) Binary tree.

• **How is binary tree represented?**

In general, each node in a binary tree contains three parts:
- Data node.
- Pointer indicating the left child.
- Pointer pointing to the right child.

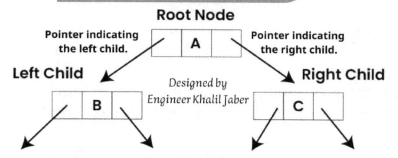

Binary Tree Representation

Root Node

Pointer indicating the left child.

A

Pointer indicating the right child.

Left Child

Right Child

Designed by Engineer Khalil Jaber

B

C

Figure (38) shows the components of the data node in the binary tree.

- **Binary tree types:** A binary tree can be classified into multiple types based on multiple factors:
- Based on the number of branches (children).
    - I.   Whole binary tree.
    - II. In. Twin apiary tree.
    - III. Dioecious trees.
- Based on completion of levels.
    - I.   Whole binary tree.
    - II. In. Perfect binary tree.
    - III. Balanced bilateral tree.
- Based on node values:
    - I.   Binary search tree
    - II. AVL tree
    - III. Red-black tree
    - IV. Tree B
    - V.   B + Tree

- **Operations on binary tree:**

- **Addition** in binary tree: We can add a node anywhere in the binary tree by adding the node as the left or right son of any node or by making the node the root of the tree.

- **Algorithm for adding** a node in a binary tree:

• Check if there is a node in the binary tree, which lost the left child. If this node exists, add the new node as its left child node.
• Check if there is a node in the binary tree, which has lost the correct child. If this node exists, add the new node as its right node.
• If we can't find any node with a missing left or right branch, find the node with two missing branches on the left or right and enter the node as a left or right subbranch.

- **Traverse** binary tree: Traversing binary tree involves visiting all binary tree nodes. Tree traversal algorithms can be broadly classified into two categories:
  • First Depth Search Algorithms (DFS).
  • Premiere search algorithms (BFS).

• First Depth Search Algorithms (DFS):

- Pass Pre-Order (Current-Left-Right): Visit the current node before visiting any nodes within the left or right subtrees. Here, the traversal is the root – the left child – the right child. This means that the root node is passed first, then its left branch and finally its right branch.
- Traverse In order (Left-Root-Right): Visit the current node after visiting all nodes within the left subtree but before visiting any node within the right subtree. Here, the traversal is the left child - the root - the right child. This means that the left child is passed first, then the root node and finally the right child.
- Post-order traverse (left to right to root): Visit the current node after visiting all the nodes in the left and right subtrees. Here, the traversal is the left child – the right child

– the root. This means that the left child has passed first, then the right child and finally the root node.

- Premiere Search Algorithms (BFS):

   Traverse the level order: Visit the nodes level by level and left to right on the same level. And here the traversal is at the level of wisdom. This means that the leftmost child has passed first and then the other children have passed from the same level from left to right.

– **Deletion** in binary tree: We can delete any node in binary tree and rearrange nodes after deletion to form a valid binary tree again.

– **Algorithm for deleting** a node in a binary tree:
• Starting at the root, find the deepest and most right node in the binary tree and the node we want to delete.
• Replace the deepest rightmost node data with the node to delete.
• Then delete the deepest node on the far right.

– **Binary tree search**: We can search for an element in the node using any of the traversal techniques.

– **Algorithm to search** for a node in a binary tree:
• Start from the root node.
• Check if the current node value is equal to the target value.
• If the current node value is equal to the target value, this node is the desired node.
• Otherwise, if the value of the node is not equal to the target value, start searching the left and right child.
• If we don't find any node whose value is equal to the target, the value does not exist in the tree.

- **The advantages of the binary tree.**

    - Effective Search: Binary trees are efficient when searching for a specific element, as each node contains at most two child nodes, allowing the use of binary search algorithms.
    - Memory efficiency: Binary trees require less memory compared to other tree data structures, and are therefore memory efficient.
    - Binary trees are relatively easy to implement and understand, as each node contains at most two children, the left child and the right child.

- **Disadvantages of a binary tree.**
    - Limited architecture: Binary trees are limited to two sub nodes per node, which may limit their usefulness in some applications. For example, if a tree requires more than two child nodes per node, a different tree structure might be more suitable.
    - Unbalanced trees: Unbalanced binary trees, where one subtree is much larger than the other, can lead to inefficient searches. This can happen if the tree is not properly balanced or if the data is inserted in non-random order.
    - Space inefficiency: Binary trees can be space-inefficient when compared to other data structures. This is because each node requires two sub-pointers, which can represent a large amount of excess memory for large trees.
    - Slow performance in worst-case scenarios: In worst-case scenarios, a binary tree can become degraded or skewed, meaning each node has only one branch. In this case, searches can deteriorate to the time complexity $O(n)$, where n is the number of nodes in the tree.

    - **Binary tree applications.**
    - The binary tree can be used to represent hierarchical data.

- Homan coding trees are used in data compression algorithms.
- A priority queue is another binary tree application that is used to search for the maximum or minimum in time complexity O(1).
- Useful for fragmented indexing in the database and useful in storing the cache in the system,
- Binary trees can be used to implement decision trees, a type of machine learning algorithm used in classification and regression analysis.

1.8.2 Binary Search Tree (BST):

It is a binary tree where each node is larger than all nodes in its left branch and smaller than all nodes in its right branch. It is a data structure used in computer science to organize and store data in an orderly manner. The binary search tree follows all the properties of the binary tree, and each node contains at most two children, a left child and a right child, where the left child contains fewer values than the original node and the right child contains greater values than the original node. This hierarchical structure allows efficient searches, additions and deletions to be performed on the data stored in the tree.

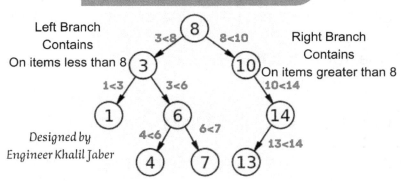

153

Figure (39) Binary Research Tree.

- **Binary search tree properties:**

- The left subtree of the node contains only nodes that have fewer keys than the node key.
- The right subtree of the node contains only nodes that have keys that are larger than the node key.
- This means that everything to the left of the root is less than the root value and everything to the right of the root is greater than the root value. Because of this performance, binary search is very easy.
- Both the left and right subtree must also be a binary search tree.
- There should be no duplicate nodes BST may have duplicate values with different processing methods to handle duplicate values in the binary search tree.
- We must follow a consistent process all the time, i.e. either the duplicate value is stored on the left or the duplicate value is stored to the right of the root.

- **Basic operations on binary search tree:**
- Find a node in BST: Means locating a specific node in the data structure. In a binary search tree, searching for a node is easy because of its specific order. The steps to find a node in the binary search tree are listed as below:
  • Compare the element to search for with the root element of the tree.
  • If the root matches the target element, return the node location.
  • If it doesn't match, check if the element is less than the root element, and if it's smaller than the root element, go to the left subtree.
  • If it is larger than the root element, go to the right subtree.

• Repeat the above procedure repeatedly until a match is found.
• If the item is not found or is not in the tree, NULL will be returned.

- **Advantages of binary search tree:**

- **Quick Find**: Searching for a specific value in BST has an average time complexity of $O(\log n)$, where n is the number of nodes in the tree. This is much faster than searching for an element in a linked array or list, which has a time complexity of $O(n)$ in the worst case.
- **Traverse in order:** BSTs can be traversed in order, visiting the left subtree, root, and right subtree. This can be used to sort the dataset.
- **Space efficient:** BSTs are space-efficient because they do not store any redundant information, unlike linked arrays and lists.

- **Disadvantages of binary research:**
  - Perverted trees: If a tree becomes skewed, the time complexity of searches, inserts, and deletions will be $O(n)$ instead of $O(\log n)$, which can render the tree inefficient.
  - Additional time required: Self-balancing trees require additional time to maintain balance during insertions and deletions.
  - Efficiency: BSTs are not effective for datasets with many iterations because they will waste space.

1.8.3 AVL tree:

It is a research binary tree in which the branches are balanced and the difference between the heights of the left subtree and the right subtree of any node is defined by the node equilibrium factor. The AVL tree is named after its inventors, Georgy Adelson-Felsky and Evgenie Landis, who published it in their 1962 paper "Algorithm for Organizing Information."

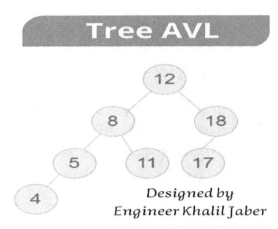

Figure (40) AVL binary tree

We can see from the previous figure that this tree is AVL because the differences between the heights of the right and left subtrees of each node are less than or equal to 1. You can also do additions, deletions or searches on the AVL tree.

- **AVL tree applications:**

- They are used to index huge records in the database and also to search them efficiently.
- AVL trees are used for all types of collections in memory, including collections and dictionaries.
- Used in database applications, where insertions and deletions are less common but frequent data searches are necessary.
- Can be used in programs that need optimal search.
- They are applied in the fields of corporate and story games.

- **Advantages of the AVL tree.**

- AVL trees can achieve self-balancing.
- It is certainly not perverted.
- Provide faster searches than red and black trees.
- The complexity of the search time is better compared to other trees such as the binary tree.
- The height cannot exceed the record (N), where N is the total number of nodes in the tree.

- **Disadvantages of the AVL tree.**

- It is difficult to implement.
- It has high stability factors for some operations.
- Less commonly used compared to red and black trees.
- Due to their fairly strict balance, AVL trees offer complex insertion and removal with more rotations.
- Take more processing to balance.

1.8.4 Red-Black Tree:

It is a research binary tree that has self-equilibrium to ensure that depth remains limited. It's a basic data structure, but its performance can be affected if a tree becomes unbalanced.

It is a type of balanced binary search tree that uses a set of rules to maintain balance, ensuring the logarithmic temporal complexity of operations such as adding, deleting, and searching, regardless of the initial shape of the tree. Red and black trees are self-balanced, using a simple color-coding system to adjust the tree after each modification.

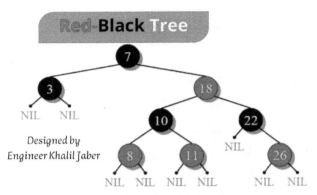

Figure (41) Red-black tree.

- **Characteristics of red and black trees:** The red-black tree has the following characteristics:

- Node color: Each Node is either red or black.
- Root Property: The root of the tree is always black.
- Red property: Red nodes cannot have red children (there are no two consecutive red nodes on any path).
- Black property: Each path from the node to its empty nodes (leaves) has the same number of black nodes.
- Sheet Feature: All NIL contract sheets are black.

These characteristics ensure that the longest path from root to leaf is only twice the shortest path, maintaining the tree's balance and effective performance.

Example of a red-black tree.

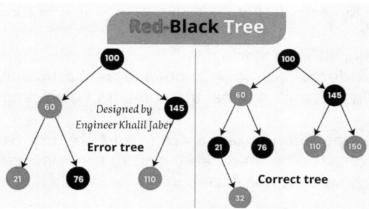

Figure (42) shows the correct red-black tree.

From the figure above, on the right side, the correct tree in red and black includes that each path from the root to the leaf node contains the same number of black nodes. In this case, there is one black node (except for the root node).

On the left, the incorrect red-black tree does not follow the characteristics of the red and black color as the red nodes are adjacent to each other. Another problem is that one path to the leaf node does not contain black nodes, while the other two paths contain a black node.

- **Comparison of the red black tree with the AVL tree:**

AVL trees are more balanced compared to red and black trees, but may cause more rotation during addition and deletion. So, if your app has frequent additions and deletions, you should prefer red and black trees. If additions and deletions are less frequent and search is more frequent, the AVL tree should be preferred over the red and black tree.

Interesting points about the red-black tree:
• The black height of the red-black tree is the number of black nodes on the path from the root node to the leaf node. Paper nodes are also counted as black nodes. So, a red-and-black tree with a height of h has a black height of > = h/2.

• The height of the red-black tree with n nodes is h<=2 log 2 (n + 1).
• All leaves (NIL) are black.
•The black depth of a node is defined as the number of black nodes from root to that node, the number of black ancestors.

- **Basic operations on a red and black tree:** Basic operations on a red and black tree include adding, searching, deleting, rotating.

- **Addition**: Adding a new node in a red and black tree involves a two-step process: first a standard binary lookup tree (BST) is added, and then enter the new node as in standard BST. The second is followed by the repair of any violations of the characteristics of the red and black color. If the new node's parent is black, no properties are violated. If the parent is red, the tree may violate the red property, requiring repairs.
- **Search**: For a node in a red and black tree is similar to searching a standard binary search tree. The search follows a direct path from root to leaf, comparing the target value to the current node value and moving left or right accordingly.
- **Deletion**: Deleting a node from a red and black tree also involves a two-step process: performing a BST deletion, followed by fixing any violations that may arise.
- **Rotation**: Rotations are essential processes in maintaining the balanced structure of the red-black (RBT) tree. They help preserve tree properties, ensuring that the longest path from root to leaf is no more than twice the length of the shortest path.

- **The advantages of trees of red and black color:**

- Balanced: Red-black trees are self-balanced, meaning they automatically maintain a balance between the heights of the

left and right subtrees. This ensures that searches, add-and-delete operations take time O(log n) in the worst case.
- Efficient search, add and delete: Due to their balanced structure, red and black trees provide efficient operations. Find, add, and delete take time O(log n) in the worst case.
- Easy to implement: the rules for maintaining the characteristics of a red-black tree are relatively simple and straightforward in execution.
- Widely used: Red-and-black trees are a popular choice for implementing various data structures, such as maps, collections, and priority queues.

- **Disadvantages of trees of red and black color:**
- More complex than other balanced trees: Compared to simpler balanced trees like AVL trees, red and black trees have more complex add and delete rules.
- Static load: Maintaining the characteristics of the red and black tree adds a simple load to each addition and deletion process.
- Not ideal for all use cases: While efficient in most operations, it may not be the best choice for applications that require frequent additions and deletions, as the static load can become significant.

- **Applications of red and black trees:**

- Implement maps and collections: Red and black trees are often used to execute maps and collections, where effective searching, adding, and deleting is crucial.
- Priority queues: Red and black trees can be used to implement priority queues, where items are ordered based on their priority.
- File systems: Red and black trees are used in some file systems to manage file and directory structures.

- In-memory databases: Red and black trees are sometimes used in in-memory databases to store and retrieve data efficiently.
- Graphics and game development: Red-Black Trees can be used to develop graphics and games for tasks such as collision detection and trajectory identification.

1.8.5 General Tree:

It is a tree in which any node can have an unlimited number of branches. In a data structure, a public tree is a tree where each node can contain zero or multiple child nodes. It cannot be empty.

In general, there is no restriction on the degree of the node. The upper node of the general tree is called the root node. There are many sub-trees in the general tree. The subtree of the public tree is unordered because the public tree nodes cannot be arranged according to specific criteria. In a public tree, each node has one inner degree (number of original nodes) and a maximum outer score (number of n sub nodes).

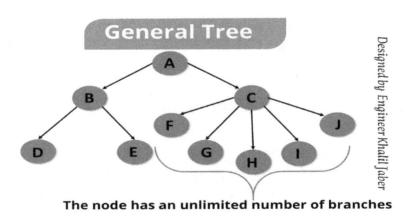

The node has an unlimited number of branches

Designed by Engineer Khalil Jaber

Figure (43) General Tree.

- **The difference between a general tree and a binary tree:**

General tree	Binary tree
A general tree is a tree in which each node can contain several children or nodes.	In a binary tree, each node can contain up to two nodes.
The subtree of the generic tree does not have the desired property.	The subtree of the binary tree retains the desired property.
In the data structure, the public tree cannot be empty.	While it can be empty.
In general, a node can contain n number of child nodes (at most)	Whereas in a binary tree, a node can contain two nodes with the number of sub nodes (at most)
In general, there is no restriction on the degree of the node.	There is a limitation to the degree of the node because nodes in the binary tree cannot contain more than two child nodes.

General tree	Binary tree
Typically, there is either a zero subtree or a multiple subtree.	While a binary tree exists, there are basically two subtrees: the left subtree and the right subtree.

- **Examples of trees with Python code.**

  - **Example 1:** Binary tree.

```python
class Node:
    def __init__(self, key):
        self.left = None
        self.right = None
        self.value = key

# To add a new node in binary tree.
def insert(root, key):
    if root is None:
        return Node(key)
    else:
        if root.value < key:
            root.right = insert(root.right, key)
        else:
            root.left = insert(root.left, key)
    return root

# To print the tree using the in-tree order (Inorder Traversal)
def inorder(root):
    if root:
        inorder(root.left)
        print(root.value)
        inorder(root.right)
```

```python
# Binary tree test
    root = Node(50)
    root = insert(root, 30)
    root = insert(root, 20)
    root = insert(root, 40)
    root = insert(root, 70)
    root = insert(root, 60)
    root = insert(root, 80)
# Print values in order within the tree
    inorder(root)
```

Example 2: Binary Search Tree

```python
    class BSTNode:
        def __init__(self, key):
            self.left = None
            self.right = None
            self.value = key
```

```python
# New node in the binary tree search
    def bst_insert(root, key):
        if root is None:
            return BSTNode(key)
        else:
            if root.value < key:
                root.right = bst_insert(root.right, key)
            else:
                root.left = bst_insert(root.left, key)
        return root
```

```python
# Function to search for value in binary tree search
    def search(root, key):
        if root is None or root.value == key:
            return root
        if root.value < key:
            return search(root.right, key)
```

```
        return search(root.left, key)
```

To print the tree using the in-tree order (Inorder Traversal)

```
    def inorder_traversal(root):
        if root:
            inorder_traversal(root.left)
            print(root.value)
            inorder_traversal(root.right)
```

Research Binary Tree Test

```
    root = BSTNode(50)
    root = bst_insert(root, 30)
    root = bst_insert(root, 20)
    root = bst_insert(root, 40)
    root = bst_insert(root, 70)
    root = bst_insert(root, 60)
    root = bst_insert(root, 80)
```

Print values in order within the tree

```
    inorder_traversal(root)
```

Find a value in the tree

```
    result = search(root, 40)
    if result:
        print(f"Value {result.value} found in the tree.")
    else:
        print("Value not found in the tree.")
```

- **Summary:**

Trees are an important data structure used in many applications such as databases, networks, and file systems. A binary tree is a common type of tree where each node has at most two branches. The search binary tree adds the sorting feature to facilitate searches. Using the codes above, we can understand how to create and use binary trees and search binary trees in Python.

- **Basic operations on trees:**

Trees are important data structures that are used in many applications. The basic operations that can be performed on trees include:

- **Insertion**: Adds a new node to the tree.
- **Deletion**: Removing a node from the tree.
- **Search**: Find a node that has a specific value in the tree.
- **Order (Traversal):** Visit all nodes in the tree in a specific order.

- **Basic operations on the binary tree in Python.**

1. Insertion: The process of adding a new node to a binary tree follows specific rules based on the node value:

- If the tree is empty, the new node becomes the root.
- If the new value is less than or equal to the value of the current node, the node is added to the left branch.
- If the new value is larger than the current node value, the node is added to the right branch.

```python
class Node:
    def __init__(self, key):
        self.left = None
        self.right = None
        self.value = key

def insert(root, key):
    if root is None:
        return Node(key)
```

```
else:
    if root.value < key:
        root.right = insert(root.right, key)
    else:
        root.left = insert(root.left, key)
return root
```

2. **Deletion**: Removing a node from a binary tree can have three states:
- The node to delete is a sheet (it has no sons).
- The node to be deleted has one son.
- The node to be deleted has two sons.

```
def delete_node(root, key):
    if root is None:
        return root

    if key < root.value:
        root.left = delete_node(root.left, key)
    elif key > root.value:
        root.right = delete_node(root.right, key)
    else:
        if root.left is None:
            return root.right
        elif root.right is None:
            return root.left

        temp = min_value_node(root.right)
        root.value = temp.value
        root.right = delete_node(root.right, temp.value)

    return root

def min_value_node(node):
    current = node
```

```
        while current.left is not None:
            current = current.left
        return current
```

3. **Search**: The process of searching for a node that contains a certain value follows the same path as the insertion operation.

```
def search(root, key):
    if root is None or root.value == key:
        return root
    if root.value < key:
        return search(root.right, key)
    return search(root.left, key)
```

4. **Arrangement (Traversal):** There are several ways to visit all the nodes in the tree:

- Inorder Traversal: Visit the left branch, then the root, then the right branch.
- Preorder Traversal: Visit the root, then the left branch, then the right branch.
- Postorder Traversal: Visit the left branch, then the right branch, then the root.

```
def inorder(root):
    if root:
        inorder(root.left)
        print(root.value, end=' ')
        inorder(root.right)

def preorder(root):
    if root:
        print(root.value, end=' ')
        preorder(root.left)
        preorder(root.right)
```

```python
def postorder(root):
    if root:
        postorder(root.left)
        postorder(root.right)
        print(root.value, end=' ')
```

- **Comprehensive practical example**: Let's write code that includes all the basic operations of the search binary tree.

```python
class BSTNode:
    def __init__(self, key):
        self.left = None
        self.right = None
        self.value = key

def bst_insert(root, key):
    if root is None:
        return BSTNode(key)
    else:
        if root.value < key:
            root.right = bst_insert(root.right, key)
        else:
            root.left = bst_insert(root.left, key)
    return root

def search(root, key):
    if root is None or root.value == key:
        return root
    if root.value < key:
        return search(root.right, key)
    return search(root.left, key)

def delete_node(root, key):
    if root is None:
        return root
```

```python
        if key < root.value:
            root.left = delete_node(root.left, key)
        elif key > root.value:
            root.right = delete_node(root.right, key)
        else:
            if root.left is None:
                return root.right
            elif root.right is None:
                return root.left

            temp = min_value_node(root.right)
            root.value = temp.value
            root.right = delete_node(root.right, temp.value)

    return root

def min_value_node(node):
    current = node
    while current.left is not None:
        current = current.left
    return current

def inorder_traversal(root):
    if root:
        inorder_traversal(root.left)
        print(root.value, end=' ')
        inorder_traversal(root.right)

def preorder_traversal(root):
    if root:
        print(root.value, end=' ')
        preorder_traversal(root.left)
        preorder_traversal(root.right)

def postorder_traversal(root):
    if root:
```

```python
        postorder_traversal(root.left)
        postorder_traversal(root.right)
        print(root.value, end=' ')
```

Process Testing.

```python
    root = BSTNode(50)
    root = bst_insert(root, 30)
    root = bst_insert(root, 20)
    root = bst_insert(root, 40)
    root = bst_insert(root, 70)
    root = bst_insert(root, 60)
    root = bst_insert(root, 80)

    print("Inorder traversal: ")
    inorder_traversal(root)
    print("\nPreorder traversal: ")
    preorder_traversal(root)
    print("\nPostorder traversal: ")
    postorder_traversal(root)

    print("n\nFind a value of 40 in the tree:")
    result = search(root, 40)
    if result:
        print(f"Value {result.value} found in the tree.")
    else:
        print("Value not found in the tree.")

    print("n\Delete node with value 20:")
    root = delete_node(root, 20)
    inorder_traversal(root)
    print("n\Delete node with a value of 30:")
    root = delete_node(root, 30)
    inorder_traversal(root)
    print("n\Delete node with value 50:")
    root = delete_node(root, 50)
    inorder_traversal(root)
```

The preceding code describes the basic operations on search binary trees, including addition, search, deletion, and multiple visits to nodes.

2.1. Definition of graphs:

They are nonlinear variable data structures used to represent relationships between objects. A graph consists of a set of points (called nodes) and a set of lines (called edges) that connect these points. The graph consists of the following:

- Vertices or Nodes: These are the objects that are represented in the graph. Heads can represent anything like people, cities, stations... Etcetera.
- Edges: They are the links that connect the headers. Edges can be directed or undirected, and can carry weights that express the strength or cost of the relationship between the heads.

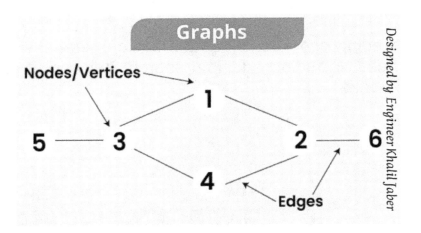

Figure (44) shows the components of the Graph.

2.2. Types of graphs:

2.2.1. **Undirected Graph:** A graph in which edges are unoriented, meaning that the relationship between any two vertices is reciprocal. That is, its edges do not contain arrows indicating the direction of traversal. Like a graph of a social network where friendships are not directional.

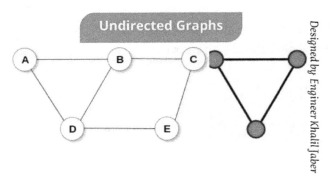

Figure (45) Undirected Graph.

2.2.2. **Directed Graph:** It is the graph in which the edges are oriented, that is, the relationship between the two vertices is not reciprocal and has a specific direction. That is, the edges have arrows indicating the direction of traversal. Such as: a web page where the links between pages are directional.

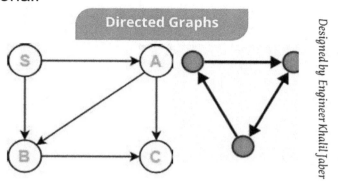

Figure (46) Directed Graph.

2.2.3. **Weighted Graph**: A graph whose edges contain weights associated with it. Weights can represent cost, distance, time.... Etcetera. Such as the road network where weights can represent the distance between two cities.

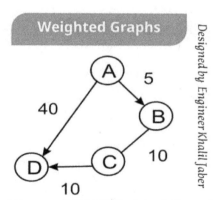

Figure (47) Weighted Graph.

2.2.4. **Unweighted Graph:** A graph whose edges do not contain weights or associated costs. Like a social network where edges represent friendships.

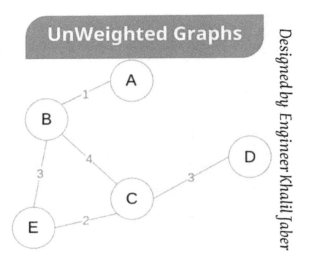

Figure (48) Unweighted Graph.

2.2.5. **Connected or Complete Graph:** A graph in which any vertex can be accessed from any other vertex across edges. That is, each peak is connected to each other peak. For example, in a tournament, each player plays against every other player.

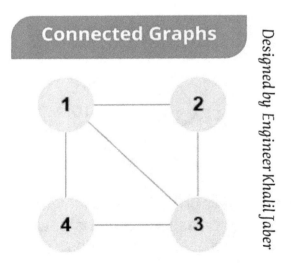

Figure (49) Connected Graph.

2.2.6. **Disconnected Graph:** A graph that contains headers that cannot be accessed from other vertices.

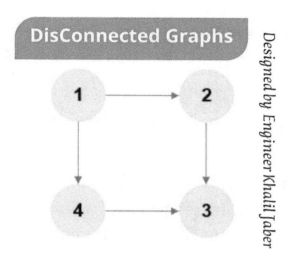

Figure (50) Disconnected Graph.

2.2.7. **Bipartite graphs** are a graph in which vertices can be divided into two separate groups so that each edge connects a vertex in one group to a vertex in the other. **Example**: Drawing a graph of the job applicant where the peaks can be divided into job applicants and job opportunities.

2.2.8. **Trees graph**: A continuous graph without cycles. **Example**: A family tree where everyone is related to their parents.

2.2.9. **Cycles**: A graph of at least one cycle. **Example**: A bicycle sharing graph where the cycles represent the paths taken by the bikes.

2.2.10.   **Spare graphs** are a graph with relatively few edges compared to the number of vertices. **Example**: A graph of a chemical reaction where each vertex represents a chemical compound and each edge represents an interaction between two compounds.

2.2.11.   **Dense Graphs**: It is a graph with many edges compared to the number of vertices. **Example**: A graph of a social network where each summit represents a person and each edge represents a friendship.

- **Example of graphs:**

- Social Networks:
- Headers: People.
- Edges: Interpersonal relationships (such as Facebook friendship).

- Road Maps:
- Vertices: cities or intersections.
- Edges: Roads connecting cities or intersections.

- Computer Networks:
- Headers: computers.
- Edges: Links (cables, wireless signals) connecting devices.

- Graph Representations of Problems:
- Headers: Represent states or points.
- Edges: Represents transitions or relationships between states.

- **Common algorithms used with Graphs.**

- Depth-First Search, DFS: Used to discover all nodes in the graph by going deeper into each branch of the graph before returning.
- Breadth-First Search, BFS: Used to discover all nodes in the graph by exploring all nodes on the same level before moving on to the next level.
- Dijkstra's Algorithm: Used to find the shortest path between two vertices in a weighted graph.

- Kruskal's Algorithm: Used to find the Minimum Spanning Tree in a weighted graph.
- Prim's Algorithm: Also used to find the lowest span tree in a weighted graph, but it starts from a given vertex and builds the tree by gradually increasing shorter edges.

2.3. How graph is represented.

- Adjacency List: Each vertex is represented by a list of adjacent headers.
- Adjacency Matrix: graphs are represented using a two-dimensional matrix where the row and column indicate vertices, and values indicate the presence or absence of an edge between the two vertices.
- **Example** of a neighborhood list: Let's consider a simple graph with 3 vertices (A, B, C) and 3 edges (A-B, B-C, A-C):

A: B, C
B: A, C
C: A, B

- **Example** of a neighborhood matrix: For the same previous graph:

A B C
A 0 1 1
B 1 0 1
C 1 1 0

Graph are one of the basic and important graphic structures that help in representing and understanding the relationships between different objects. They can be used in multiple fields such as social networks, transportation routes, computer networks, and even in solving mathematical and complex problems.

2.4. What are the characteristics of graphs.

Graphs are robust and flexible data structures, with several characteristics that distinguish them from other data structures. Here are some key characteristics of graph:

- Vertices or Nodes and edges.
  - Headers: represent different objects or elements.
  - Edges: represent the relationships or connections between the vertices.

- Direction:
  - Undirected Graph: The edges are unoriented, meaning that the relationship between any two vertices is reciprocated.
  - Directed Graph: The edges are oriented, meaning that the relationship between the two vertices has a specific direction.

- Weights:
  - Weighted Graph: Edges contain weights that express the cost, distance, or strength of the relationship.
  - Unweighted Graph: Edges do not contain weights.

- Connectivity:
  - Connected Graph: Accessible from any vertex to any other.
  - Disconnected Graph: Contains headers that cannot be accessed from other vertices.

- Cycles:
  - Cyclic Graph: Contains one or more cycles, where you can refer to the same vertex via a specific path.
  - Acyclic Graph: does not contain any cycles.

- Degree
- Degree of a vertex: The number of edges attached to the head.
- In-degree: In oriented graph, it is the number of edges that enter the header.
- Out-degree: In oriented graph, it is the number of edges that come out of the vertex.

- Repetition (Multiplicity)
- Simple Graph: Does not have duplicate edges or self-rings (edges that connect the head to itself).
- Multigraph: Contains duplicate edges between the same pairs of vertices.
- Self-loop Graph: Contains edges that connect the head to itself.

- Minimum Spanning Tree.
- Lowest span tree: It is a continuous subtree that contains all the vertices and the sum of its edge weights is the lowest.

- Harmonics (Cliques)
- Harmonics: A group of vertices in the graph where each vertex is connected to all other vertices in the group.

- Paths
- Path: A sequence of vertices where from one vertex to another is reached across edges.
- Simple path: A path that does not contain duplicate headers.
- Longest Path: The longest simple path between two vertices in the graph.

- Shortest Path: The shortest path between two vertices in the graph.

- **Conclusion:** Graphs provide a powerful and flexible way to represent relationships between different objects. Understanding the properties of graphs helps in choosing the right algorithms and techniques to solve problems involving complex relationships between elements.

2.5. Graphs features.

- Representation of complex relationships: graphs can represent relationships between elements in an efficient and flexible way, making them suitable for modeling social networks, computer networks, transportation routes, and more.
- Efficient navigation: Graphs enable search and navigation between elements effectively using algorithms such as Occasional Search (BFS) and Deep Search (DFS).
- Find optimal paths: Graphs can be used to find the shortest paths between points using algorithms such as Dijkstra's Algorithm and Floyd-Warshall Algorithm.
- Minimum Span Tree: Graphs enable the construction of a minimum span tree that connects all points at the lowest possible cost using algorithms such as Kruskal's Algorithm and Prim's Algorithm.
- Versatility: Graphs are versatile and can be adapted for a wide range of applications, including science, engineering, networking, artificial intelligence, and data analysis.

2.6. Disadvantages of Graphs.

- Time complexity: Operations on Graphs, such as finding the shortest route or finding the lowest spanning tree, can be time-prohibitive especially on large graphs.
- Spatial complexity: Storing graphs can be space-costly, especially when using an Adjacency Matrix that requires space where ($O(V^2)$) is the number of vertices.
- Maintenance: Updating graphs and adding or removing headers or edges can be complex and takes time and effort.
- Big data management: Dealing with graphs with a large number of vertices and edges can be challenging in terms of performance and efficiency.
- Representation and analysis: Correctly representing and analyzing graphs can be difficult, especially if the relationships between the elements are complex or multifaceted.

- **Conclusion:** Graphs is a powerful and useful tool for representing complex relationships between elements, and provides many advantages such as effective representation of relationships, effective navigation, and finding optimal paths. However, temporal, spatial and big data management complexities must be considered when working with Graphs to ensure performance and efficiency.

Graphs are used programmatically in a wide range of applications and domains where relationships between objects and elements are essential. Here are some examples and common cases where Graphs are used:

- Social Networks.
- Representation: individuals as a contract and social relations as edges.
- Usage: analysis of social networks, suggestion of friends, discovery of communities.

- Computer Networks.
- Representation: devices as nodes and the connections between them as edges.
- Usage: Finding optimal routes for data transfer, network analysis, detecting attacks.

- Graphs and Routes.
- Representation: cities or intersections as nodes and roads as edges.
- Usage: trip planning, finding shorter routes, traffic management.

- AI and Machine Learning.
- Representation: Representation of game states or environments as nodes and movements or transitions as edges.
- Usage: Algorithms for searching for pathways, optimizations, analysis of neural networks.

- Project Management.
- Representation: tasks as nodes and temporal relationships or dependency as edges.
- Usage: project planning, critical path analysis, timeline optimization.

- Biology and Bioinformatics.
- Metabolism: proteins or genes as nodes and biological reactions as edges.
- Usage: analysis of biological networks, study of protein interactions, detection of diseases.

- Text Analysis and Semantic Networks.

- Representation: words or concepts as nodes and semantic relationships as edges.
- Usage: Natural language processing, semantic relationship analysis, knowledge extraction.

- Video Games.
- Representation: states or places in the game as nodes and movements or tracks as edges.
- Usage: Plan moves, find optimal paths, design game levels.

- Financial Networks Analysis.
- Representation: institutions or individuals as a contract and financial transactions as edges.
- Usage: pattern detection, risk analysis, financial fraud detection.

- Big Data and Network Analysis.
- Representation: objects or events as nodes and relationships or interactions as edges.
- Usage: Big Data Analysis, Pattern Detection, Big Social Network Analysis.

- **Conclusion:** Graphs are used programmatically in a wide range of domains that require representation of relationships and interactions between objects or elements. The choice of using graphs depends on the structural nature of the relationships between objects and the ability to take advantage of the analysis and associated relationships to achieve the desired goals. In Python, graphs can be represented using several methods, the most famous of which are the use of the Adjacency List and the Adjacency Matrix.

- Here is an explanation of how graphs are represented by these two methods with code examples:

1. Represent graphs using Adjacency List A neighborhood list is a space-effective way to represent graphs, where each vertex is stored with a list of adjacent headers.
Example:

```
class Graph:
    def __init__(self):
        self.graph{} =

    def add_edge(self, u, v):
        if u not in self.graph:
            self.graph[u][] =
        if v not in self.graph:
            self.graph[v][] =
        self.graph[u].append(v)
        self.graph[v].append(u) # if the map is not oriented

    def display(self):
        for vertex in self.graph:
            print(f"{vertex}: {self.graph[vertex]}")
```

Create Graphs
```
    g = Graph()
    g.add_edge("A", "B")
    g.add_edge("A", "C")
    g.add_edge("B", "C")
    g.add_edge("B", "D")
```

View Graphs
```
    g.display()
```

Expected result:

A: ['B', 'C']
B: ['A', 'C', 'D']
C: ['A', 'B']
D: ['B']

2. Graph representation using the neighborhood matrix (Adjacency Matrix) A neighborhood matrix is another way to represent graphs, where a two-dimensional matrix is used to store information about the presence of edges between vertices.

Example:

```
class Graph:
    def __init__(self, num_vertices):
        self.num_vertices = num_vertices
        self.graph = [[0 for _ in range(num_vertices)] for _ in range(num_vertices)]

    def add_edge(self, u, v):
        self.graph[u][v] = 1  # If graph is not directed

    def display(self):
        for row in self.graph:
            print(row)
```

 # Create Graphs
```
g = Graph(4)
g.add_edge(1 ,0)
g.add_edge(2 ,0)
g.add_edge(2 ,1)
g.add_edge(3 ,1)
```

 # View Graphs
```
g.display()
```

 # Expected result:

```
[0 ,1 ,1 ,0]
[1 ,1 ,0 ,1]
[0 ,0 ,1 ,1]
[0 ,0 ,1 ,0]
```

3. Graph representation using the 'networkx' library is a powerful and flexible library for working with graphs in Python. This library provides many useful functions for creating and manipulating graphs.

Example:

```
import networkx as nx
import matplotlib.pyplot as plt
```

Create Graphs

```
G = nx.Graph()
G.add_edge("A", "B")
G.add_edge("A", "C")
G.add_edge("B", "C")
G.add_edge("B", "D")
```

View Graphs

```
print("Nodes:", G.nodes())
print("Edges:", G.edges())
```

Graph drawing

```
nx.draw(G, with_labels=True)
plt.show()
```

Expected result:

```
Nodes: ['A', 'B', 'C', 'D']
Edges: [('A', 'B'), ('A', 'C'), ('B', 'C'), ('B', 'D')]
```

Note here that the graph shows the vertices and edges.

• **Conclusion**: In Python, graphs can be represented using several methods depending on the nature of graph and application requirements. Using the neighborhood list and the neighborhood array are basic methods, while the 'networkx' library provides a user-friendly interface with many useful functions for processing graphs.

- These are Python programs that give graphs.

For sure! The 'networkx' library can be used in collaboration with the 'matplotlib' library in Python to create a graph. Here's how to do it:

Graph drawing using 'networkx' and 'matplotlib'

```
import networkx as nx
import matplotlib.pyplot as plt
```

Create a new graph

```
G = nx.Graph()
```

Add headers (Nodes)

```
G.add_nodes_from(["A", "B", "C", "D"])
```

Add edges

```
G.add_edges_from([("A", "B"), ("A", "C"), ("B", "C"), ("B", "D")])
```

Graph drawing

```
pos = nx.spring_layout(G) # Specify layout shape
nx.draw(G, pos, with_labels=True, node_size=700,
node_color='skyblue', font_size=15, font_color='black',
font_weight='bold', edge_color='gray')
```

View drawing
```
plt.title("Graph Visualization")
```

```
plt.show()
```

Code Explanation:

1. Import libraries:
   - 'networkx' to create and manipulate graphs.
   - 'matplotlib.pyplot' to draw graph.

2. Create a new graph:
   - 'G = nx. Graph()' creates a new undirected graph.

3. Add headers:
   - 'G.add_nodes_from(["A", "B", "C", "D"])' adds headers to the graph.

4. Add edges:
   - 'G.add_edges_from([("A", "B"), ("A", "C"), ("B", "C"), ("B", "D")])' adds edges between headers.

5. Graph drawing:
   - 'pos = nx.spring_layout(G)' uses the spring planning algorithm to determine the positions of vertices.
   - 'nx.draw(G, pos, with_labels=True, node_size=700, node_color='skyblue', font_size=15, font_color='black', font_weight='bold', edge_color='gray')' draws graph with headers and edges with color and size configuration.

6. Graphic Width:
   - 'plt.title("Graph Visualization")' adds a title to the drawing.
   - 'plt.show()' displays the drawing.

- **Result**: The resulting graphic will be an illustration graph containing the headers "A", "B", "C", "D" with the edges connecting them, and the graphics clearly illustrate the relationships.

- Customize the graphic: You can customize the graphic as needed by changing the colors, sizes, and edge styles. Here is an example with some additional customizations:

```
import networkx as nx
import matplotlib.pyplot as plt
```

Create a new graph

```
G = nx.Graph()
```

Add headers (Nodes)

```
G.add_nodes_from(["A", "B", "C", "D"])
```

Add edges

```
G.add_edges_from([("A", "B"), ("A", "C"), ("B", "C"), ("B", "D")])
```

Graph drawing

```
pos = nx.spring_layout(G) # Specify layout shape
nx.draw(G, pos, with_labels=True, node_size=700,
node_color='lightgreen', font_size=15, font_color='black',
font_weight='bold', edge_color='blue', width=2.0)
```

Add labels on edges

```
edge_labels = {("A", "B"): "A-B", ("A", "C"): "A-C", ("B", "C"): "B-C", ("B",
"D"): "B-D"}
nx.draw_networkx_edge_labels(G, pos, edge_labels=edge_labels,
font_color='red')
```

View drawing

```
plt.title("Customized Graph Visualization")
```

```
plt.show()
```
This way, you can easily create graphs using Python and the 'networkx' library.

End of chapter 3

# Chapter 4:

❏ *Immutable (Static)Data Structures.*

1. **Records.**
2. **Array.**
3. **Arrays tow dim.**
4. **Tables.**

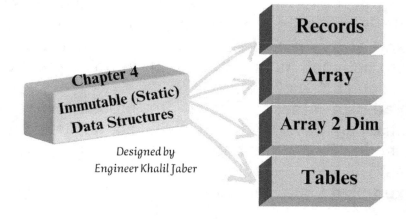

1.1. What are static data structures?

These are data structures whose size is fixed and cannot be changed after they are created. The size of these structures is determined when they are created, and elements of them cannot be added or removed from them afterwards. Here are some common types of static data structures:

1.2. Common Types of static data structures.

1.2.1. **Arrays**: A collection of similar elements that are stored in successive locations in memory. Items are accessed using an index. The size of the array must be specified when it is created and cannot be changed afterwards.
1.2.2. **Fixed arrays** (Fixed-size Arrays): Like regular arrays but more common in languages that do not support dynamic resizing such as C.
1.2.3. **Fixed-size stacks:** These are predetermined stacks. Items can be added and removed according to LIFO (Last In, First Out) rules, but cannot be resized after creation.
1.2.4. **Fixed-size Lists:** Similar to arrays but may have different interfaces to handle. Their size is fixed and cannot be changed.

1.3. Features of static data structures:

- **Performance**: Since its size is fixed, memory can be allocated more efficiently.
- **Simplicity**: They are simpler than dynamic structures where memory allocation and editing management is not required.
- **Stability**: Provides consistent performance because the size does not change.

1.4. Disadvantages of static data structures:

- Limited flexibility: cannot be resized to meet changing data needs.
- Memory waste: If more volume is allocated than required, memory wasting may occur.

Static data structures are suitable for use in cases where the volume of data is known in advance and does not change over time.

❑ **Static Data Structures**
1. Records.

1.1. Definition of Records:

A record is a set of values related to each other that are stored together as a single unit. A record is typically used to represent a specific entity or thing in programming, such as information about a student or employee.

It is considered a static data structure. A record is a type of data structure that combines a number of values that may be of different data types under a single name. Each value within the record is called a field, and these fields can be of different data types such as integers, texts, etc.

1.2. Features of records:

- Data organization: It helps organize data that are related to each other into a single structure.
- Direct Access: Any field within the record is easily accessible by field name.
- Group different data: A record can contain fields of different data types, making it convenient to collect various data related to a single object.

1.3. Disadvantages of Records:

- Fixed volume: Like other static data structures, the size of a record is fixed after it is created.
- Extensibility: If you need to add new fields to the record, this may require redefining the record and reallocating memory.

1.4. Example of records: In Python, records can be defined using class. You can define a class that contains the different fields that you want to include in the record. Here's an example of how to define a record that represents student information:

```python
class Student:
    def __init__(self, student_id, name, grade):
        self.student_id = student_id
        self.name = name
        self.grade = grade
```

Create an object from the student class

```python
student1 = Student(1, "Ahmed", 90.5)
```

Access log fields

```python
print(f"ID: {student1.student_id}")
print(f"Name: {student1.name}")
print(f"Grade: {student1.grade}")
```

In this example, a class named 'Student' is defined and contains three fields: 'student_id', 'name', and 'grade'. The '__init__' function is defined to specify how to create an object from this class and assign values to the fields. Next, an object is created from the class 'Student' and values are assigned to the fields. Fields can be accessed using '.' (period) following the object name.

Using class in Python, you can define complex records that contain a variety of fields and different data types.

In data structures, records are represented in different ways depending on the language or software environment used. Generally, records can be represented using several common methods such as classes, tuples, dictionaries in Python. We will discuss each method in detail with examples.

- The use of classes is the most obvious way to represent records in object-oriented programming.

```python
class Student:
    def __init__(self, student_id, name, grade):
        self.student_id = student_id
        self.name = name
        self.grade = grade
```

Create an object from the Student class

```python
student1 = Student(1, "Ahmed", 90.5)
```

Access record fields

```python
print(f"ID: {student1.student_id}")
print(f"Name: {student1.name}")
print(f"Grade: {student1.grade}")
```

- Use tuples: It is a simple and light way to represent records if the fields are few and the number is known in advance.

Definition of tuple represents a student

```python
student = (1, "Ahmed", 90.5)
```

Access fields using the index
```python
print(f"ID: {student[0]}")
print(f"Name: {student[1]}")
print(f"Grade: {student[2]}")
```

- Use dictionaries: Provides a flexible way to store records using key/value pairs.

Dictionary definition representing a student

```python
student = {
    "student_id": 1,
    "name": "Ahmed",
    "grade": 90.5 }
```

Access fields using the key

```python
print(f"ID: {student['student_id']}")
print(f"Name: {student['name']}")
print(f"Grade: {student['grade']}")
```

- Using namedtuple: In Python, 'namedtuple' from the 'collections' library provides a flexible and lightweight way to represent records.

```python
from collections import namedtuple
```

Define namedtuple represents a student

```python
Student = namedtuple('Student', ['student_id', 'name', 'grade'])
```

Create an object from namedtuple

```python
student1 = Student(1, "Ahmed", 90.5)
```

Access fields using names

```python
print(f"ID: {student1.student_id}")
print(f"Name: {student1.name}")
print(f"Grade: {student1.grade}")
```

- Using Data Classes (in Python) is a new feature in Python that provides a simple and efficient way to represent records.

```python
from dataclasses import dataclass

@dataclass
class Student:
    student_id: int
    name: str
    grade: float
```

Create an object from the student class

```python
student1 = Student(1, "Ahmed", 90.5)
```

Access fields

```python
print(f"ID: {student1.student_id}")
print(f"Name: {student1.name}")
print(f"Grade: {student1.grade}")
```

Each of these methods has its advantages and disadvantages, and choosing the right method depends on the needs of the particular application and the programming context. Records are used in data structures when there is a need to aggregate a set of values related to each other into a single structure. Logs are useful in several situations, including:

- Representation of complex entities: When you need to represent an entity that contains a set of different attributes or data, such as:
- Employee: Contains employee ID, name, salary, and job title.
- Student: Contains student ID, name, grade, and age.
- Quick and direct access to data: Records provide quick access to different values using field names, making it easier to read and write data.

- Organize data in databases: Records are widely used in databases to organize data into tables, where each record represents a row in the table.
- Handling input and output data: When reading or writing data from files or receiving data from APIs, different values are grouped into logs for easy processing.
- Data representation in large applications: In large, complex applications, records help organize data in an organized and logical manner, facilitating maintenance and application expansion.

- **Examples of using a record:**

- **Student Management App:** Records can be used to store student data:

```
from dataclasses import dataclass

@ dataclass
class Student:
    student_id: int
    name: str
        grade: float
            age: int

Students = [
    Student(1, "Ahmed", 90.5, 20),
    Student(2, "Sara", 85.0, 22),
    Student(3, "Ali", 78.0, 19) ]
```

Access student data

```
for student in students:
```

```python
        print(f"ID: {student.student_id}, Name:
{student.name}, Grade: {student.grade}, Age:
{student.age}")
```

- **Employee management app:** Records can be used to store employee data:

```python
from dataclasses import dataclass

@  dataclass
  class Employee:
     employee_id: int
     name: str
     salary: float
     position: str

  employees = [
     Employee(1, "Ahmed", 50000.0, "Developer"),
     Employee(2, "Sara", 60000.0, "Manager"),
     Employee(3, "Ali", 45000.0, "Designer") ]
```

Access to employee data

```python
  for employee in employees:
     print(f"ID: {employee.employee_id}, Name:
{employee.name}, Salary: {employee.salary}, Position:
{employee.position}")
```

- **Benefits:**

- Clarity: Makes the code clearer and more organized.
- Maintainability: Facilitates code maintenance and expansion by adding new fields to the record.
- Efficiency: Provides an effective means of organizing and storing linked data.

- **Conclusion**: Using records in data structures is an excellent option when you need to group a set of related values into a single structure, making handling data more organized and clearer.

Here is now a complete software application in Python that shows how to use records using class to organize and manage student data.

Application for student data management.

```python
from dataclasses import dataclass, field
from typing import List

@dataclass
class Student:
    student_id: int
    name: str
    grade: float
    age: int

Class StudentManageSystem:
    Dave __Innet__(predecessor):
        Ancestor.students: NotstudentNet = []

    def add_student(self, student: Student):
        self.students.append(student)
        print(f"Added student: {student.name}")

    def remove_student(self, student_id: int):
        student_to_remove = None
        for student in self.students:
            if student.student_id == student_id:
                student_to_remove = student
                break
```

```python
        if student_to_remove:
            self.students.remove(student_to_remove)
            print(f"Removed student:
{student_to_remove.name}")
        else:
            print(f"Student with ID {student_id} not found")

    def display_students(self):
        if not self.students:
            print("No students to display")
        else:
            for student in self.students:
                print(f"ID: {student.student_id}, Name:
{student.name}, Grade: {student.grade}, Age:
{student.age}")
```

Create a student management system

```python
sms = StudentManagementSystem()
```

Add some students

```python
    sms.add_student(Student(1, "Ahmed", 90.5, 20))
    sms.add_student(Student(2, "Sara", 85.0, 22))
    sms.add_student(Student(3, "Ali", 78.0, 19))
```

View student list

```python
    print("\nList of students:")
    sms.display_students()
```

Remove a student

```python
    sms.remove_student(2)
```

View list of students after removal

```
print("\nList of students after removal:")
sms.display_students()
```

Explanation of the application

- Definition of Student:
- Contains fields: 'student_id', 'name', 'grade', and 'age'.
- '@dataclass' is used to simplify the definition of class.

- StudentManagementSystem Class:
- Contains a list of students ('students').
- Provides ways to add students ('add_student'), remove students ('remove_student'), and view the list of students ('display_students').

- Create an object from the Student Management System (SMS):
- Some students are created and added to the system.
- The list of students is displayed.
- A caller is removed and list is displayed again to clarify the changes.

Run the application: When you run this program, the result will be as follows:

```
Added student: Ahmed
Added student: Sara
Added student: Ali

List of students:
ID: 1, Name: Ahmed, Grade: 90.5, Age: 20
ID: 2, Name: Sara, Grade: 85.0, Age: 22
```

ID: 3, Name: Ali, Grade: 78.0, Age: 19

Removed student: Sara

List of students after removal:
ID: 1, Name: Ahmed, Grade: 90.5, Age: 20
ID: 3, Name: Ali, Grade: 78.0, Age: 19

From this app, you can see how to use records to organize and manage student data easily and effectively.

□ **Static Data Structures**
2. Arrays.

2.1. What is Array?

Array is a data structure in programming used to store a set of elements that are similar in type. Also known as the matrix. Array has the following characteristics:

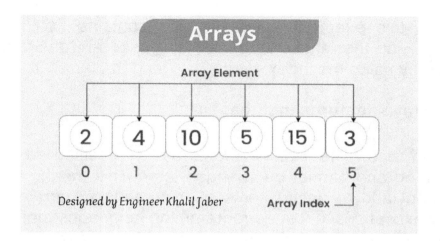

Designed by Engineer Khalil Jaber

Figure (51) Matrix or Array.

- Cascading storage: Items are stored in successive locations in memory.
- Random access: Any item can be accessed directly using its index.
- Single type: All elements in array are of the same type (for example, all elements are integers or all text).
- Fixed size: The size of the array is specified when it is created and cannot be changed later (in some programming languages there are other types that allow resizing).

\# **Example** of array in the Python programming language:
\# Array definition contains 5 elements.

```
arr = [1, 2, 3, 4, 5]
```

\# Access items using the index

```
for i in range(len(arr)):
    print(f"Element at index {i} is {arr[i]}")
```

In this example, an array that contains five items is defined, and then those items are accessed and their value is printed by using the index.

2.2. Array's features include:

- Fixed size: The size of the array is specified when it is created and cannot be changed later. This means that you cannot add or delete items after creating an array. (There are exceptions in some programming languages that provide dynamic arrays such as 'ArrayList' in Java or 'vector' in C++).
- Single type: All elements in array are of the same type (such as all elements are integers or all text).
- Random access: Any item can be accessed directly using its index, making reads and writes fast and almost constant in time ($O(1)$).
- Cascading storage: Items are stored in successive locations in memory. This allows quick access to items but can be constrained in terms of efficiency at times when the array needs to be oversized.
- Efficiency in terms of memory consumption: Since array requires consecutive memory storage, memory management is effective, and there is no wasted space between the elements. However, the full size of the array must be allocated in advance, which can lead to memory waste if the allocated size is larger than required.
- Simplicity in use: Arrays are simple and easy to use in programming, making them suitable for basic and simple applications.
- Performance: Performance in accessing items is excellent ($O(1)$), but performance in insertion and removal operations can be poor, especially if the process requires moving a lot of items.

- No built-in operations: In traditional static arrays, there are no built-in operations to add or delete items or to increase the size of the array. But there are dynamic arrays in some languages that provide these operations such as 'ArrayList' in Java and 'vector' in C++.

An example of some of these properties:
Random Access:
Define arrays in Python.

```
arr = [10, 20, 30, 40, 50]
```

Access the third item (index 2)

```
print(arr[2])      # will print 30
```

These are some of the basic properties of Arrays in data structures.

2.3. Arrays Features:

- Quick access (O(1)): You can quickly access any element in an array using its index. This makes reading and writing operations fast and time-consistent.
- Simplicity and ease: Arrays are simple, easy to understand and use. It only requires knowing the size when creating and the type of elements.
- Contiguous memory: Objects are stored in successive locations in memory, which can improve performance due to CPU and cache-level optimizations.
- Memory efficiency: There is no memory wasted between the elements because they are all stored consecutively.
- Stability in size: Setting the array size in advance prevents unwanted changes in size, which can be an advantage in

some applications that require careful resource management.

2.4. Disadvantages of Arrays:

- Fixed size: The array cannot be resized after it is created. If you need flexibility in size, it may be necessary to use dynamic data structures such as Linked Lists or dynamic arrays.
- Difficulty inserting and removing: Adding or removing items usually requires moving many other items, making these operations slow (O(n)).
- Single type: All elements in the array must be of the same type, which can be restrictive in some cases.
- Potential memory waste: If larger than required volume is allocated, there can be memory waste.
- Static memory management: The need to know the size of the array in advance can be inconvenient in cases where the amount of data to be stored cannot be predicted.

Example of array features in Python:

```
arr = [1, 2, 3, 4, 5]
print(arr[2]) # quick access: print the third item
```

Example of array flaws in Python:

```
arr = [1, 2, 3, 4, 5]
```

To add a new item, you need to create a new array with a larger size

```
arr.append (6)
```

This requires a copy of elements in memory if memory reallocation is needed.

In this example, we see how quickly an element can be accessed in array, but adding a new element may require a copy operation for the elements in case memory needs to be reallocated, illustrating one of the potential drawbacks of arrays.

2.5. When is Arrays used?

Array is used in many cases due to its features, and the following are some common scenarios in which array is used:

2.5.1. When quick access to items is needed: If applications require quick and frequent access to items based on the index, array is the appropriate option. For example, in games, arrays can be used to store object coordinates for quick access.

2.5.2. When the data size is already known: If you already know how many items you'll be dealing with, array is convenient for storing this data. For example, store student grades in a class where the number of students is known.

2.5.3. To improve performance and utilize cascading memory: Sequential storage of objects in memory can improve performance thanks to the utilization of CPU and cache optimizations.

2.5.4. For static applications: In applications where data doesn't change much after it's created, array is a good choice. For example, store the names of the days of the week or the months of the year.

2.5.5. To handle simple data: Array is very convenient for storing simple and direct data such as numbers and texts. For example, store a list of prime numbers or a list of capitals.

2.5. 6. When quick searches are needed: Array is useful in operations that require quick search for items using the index.

2.5.7. In algorithms and numerical processing: Arrays are widely used in various algorithms and numerical processing, such as mathematical processing, instant transformations, and digital signal processing.

Examples of using Arrays:
  - Storing students' grades:

grades = [85, 90, 78, 92, 88] # Grades per class

  - Store the coordinates of objects in a game:

x_coordinates = [10, 20, 30, 40]
y_coordinates = [15, 25, 35, 45]

In these examples, arrays are used to store predefined data and require quick and frequent access to items.

- A comprehensive programming example in Python: Explains how to define Arrays, access elements in them, modify their values, add elements to them, or remove items from them:

Arrays definition

arr = [10, 20, 30, 40, 50]

Print the original array

print("original vector:", arr)

Access items

```python
print("Item at index 0:", arr[0])
print("Item at index 2:", arr[2])
print("Item at index 4:", arr[4])
```

Modify values.

```python
arr[2] = 35
print("array after modifying the element at index 2:", arr)
```

Add items

```python
arr.append(60)
print("array after adding element 60:", arr)
```

Remove items

```python
arr.remove(20)
print("array after removing element 20:", arr)
```

Array length

```python
print("length array :", len(arr))
```

Pass over all items using a loop

```python
print("Array elements:")
for i in range(len(arr)):
print(f"element at index {i}: {arr[i]}")
```

Search for an item in Array

```python
search_value = 40
if search_value in arr:
print(f"element {search_value} exists in Array at index
{arr.index(search_value)}")
```

```
else:
    print(f"element {search_value} does not exist in Array")
```

Sort Array

```
arr.sort()
print("Array after sorting:", arr)
```

Reverse the order of items in Array

```
arr.reverse()
print("Array after reverse order:", arr)
```

❑ Static Data Structures
3. Arrays Tow Dim.

3.1. What is Array Tow Dim?

Two-dimensional arrays are a type of data structure in which elements are organized into a grid or a table with rows and columns. This type of matrix can be useful for representing tables, mathematical matrices, images, or any other data that can be divided into two dimensions.

3.2. Definition of a two-dimensional array.

A two-dimensional matrix is defined as a matrix that contains other matrices as its components. In other words, every element in a base matrix is actually another matrix. This can be visualized as a matrix of rows, where each row is an individual matrix.

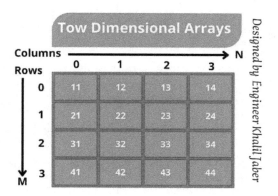

Figure (52) Two-dimensional Array.

General representation: The two-dimensional matrix is known as M x N, where M is the number of rows and N is the number of columns. They can be represented as follows:

Definition of a two-dimensional matrix MxN.

```
array = [
    ['a11', 'a12', 'a13', '...', 'a1N'],
    ['a21', 'a22', 'a23', '...', 'a2N'],
    ['a31', 'a32', 'a33', '...', 'a3N'],
    ['aM1', 'aM2', 'aM3', '...', 'aMN']
]
```

Array printing

```
        Print("Two-dimensional array:")
        For Row in Array:
            For Element in Row:
                Print(Element, End =" ")
            Print()
```

Calculate the average of rows and columns (by default counts will be used for better analysis) Now let's say we're dealing with numbers instead of symbols:

Array Numbers

```
array = [
    [11, 12, 13, 14],
    [21, 22, 23, 24],
    [31, 32, 33, 34],
    [41, 42, 43, 44]
]
```

Matrix printing

```
Print ("two-dimensional array:")
For Row in Array:
    For Element in Row:
        Print(Element, End =" ")
    Print()
```
Calculate the average of each row

```
print("nAverage per row:")
for i, row in enumerate(array):
    average = sum(row) / len(row)
    print(f"row {i + 1}: {average:.2f}")
```

Calculate the average of each column

```
num_rows = len(array)
num_cols = len(array[0])

print("naverage each column:")
for j in range(num_cols):
    col_total = sum(array[i][j] for i in range(num_rows))
    col_average = col_total / num_rows
```

```python
        print(f"column{j + 1}: {col_average:.2f}")
```

Full Program
Definition of a two-dimensional array MxN with numbers

```python
    array = [
        [11, 12, 13, 14],
        [21, 22, 23, 24],
        [31, 32, 33, 34],
        [41, 42, 43, 44]
    ]
```

Matrix printing

```python
        Print("Two-dimensional array:")
        For Row in Array:
            For Element in Row:
                Print(Element, End =" ")
            Print()
```
Calculate the average of each row

```python
        print("n/Average per row:")
        for i, row in enumerate(array):
            average = sum(row) / len(row)
            print(f"row {i + 1}: {average:.2f}")
```

Calculate the average of each column

```python
        num_rows = len(array)
        num_cols = len(array[0])

        print("n/average each column:")
        for j in range(num_cols):
            col_total = sum(array[i][j] for i in range(num_rows))
            col_average = col_total / num_rows
            print(f"column{j + 1}: {col_average:.2f}")
```

Access to array elements: Any element in a two-dimensional array can be accessed using two pointers: the first points to the row, the second indicates the column. For example, to access the item in row i and column j:

```
element = array[i][j]
```

Create a two-dimensional array

Create a 3x3 array

```
array = [
    [1, 2, 3],
    [4, 5, 6],
    [7, 8, 9]
]
```

Matrix printing

```
for row in array:
    for element in row:
        print(element, end=" ")
    print()
```

Operations on two-dimensional arrays.

Iteration across array elements: You can iterate across all array elements using two nested loops. In Python:

```
for i in range(len(array)):
    for j in range(len(array[i])):
        print(array[i][j], end=" ")
    print()
```

Addition or subtraction of two arrays: Two two-dimensional arrays can be added or subtracted by adding or subtracting the corresponding elements into the two arrays. For example, to add two arrays:

```python
def add_matrices(matrix1, matrix2):
    result = []
    for i in range(len(matrix1)):
        row = []
        for j in range(len(matrix1[i])):
            row.append(matrix1[i][j] + matrix2[i][j])
        result.append(row)
    return result

        matrix1 = [
            [1, 2, 3],
            [4, 5, 6],
            [7, 8, 9]
        ]
        matrix2 = [
            [9, 8, 7],
            [6, 5, 4],
            [3, 2, 1]
        ]

        result = add_matrices(matrix1, matrix2)
        print(result)
```

Multiplying two matrices: Multiplying two-dimensional matrices requires calculating the sum of the product of the elements of rows by columns. In Python:

```python
def multiply_matrices(matrix1, matrix2):
    result = [[0 for _ in range(len(matrix2[0]))]
 for _ in range(len(matrix1))]
    for i in range(len(matrix1)):
```

```
    for j in range(len(matrix2[0])):
        for k in range(len(matrix2)):
            result[i][j] += matrix1[i][k] * matrix2[k][j]
return result

    matrix1 = [
        [1, 2, 3],
        [4, 5, 6],
        [7, 8, 9]
    ]

    matrix2 = [
        [9, 8, 7],
        [6, 5, 4],
        [3, 2, 1]
    ]

result = multiply_matrices(matrix1, matrix2)
print(result)
# Practical applications
```

- Graphs: Two-dimensional matrices can be used to represent images, where each element in the matrix represents pixels with its color.
- Spreadsheets: Used to represent attributes such as database tables or spreadsheets in programs such as Excel.
- Mathematical matrices: used to solve algebraic equations, applications of linear algebra, and statistics.

3.3. What are the properties of Array tow dim?

Two-dimensional arrays have many important properties that make them useful in many applications. Here are some of these characteristics:

3.3.1. Organization in the form of a table: Items are organized into rows and columns, making it easier to access and process data into an organized structure.

3.3.2. Direct access: Any element in the array can be accessed directly using two pointers, one for the row and one for the column, providing quick access to the data.

3.3.3. Store homogeneous data: Two-dimensional arrays store data of the same type, making them suitable for storing homogeneous data such as numbers or letters.

3.3.4. Persistent memory: In many programming languages, arrays are stored in continuous memory, facilitating quick and efficient access to elements using simple calculations of memory locations.

3.3.5. Iteration and grouping: Operations on rows or columns can be performed separately, allowing many algorithms to be implemented effectively such as find, filtering, and grouping algorithms.

3.3.6. Support mathematical operations: Two-dimensional matrices can be used in mathematical operations, such as adding matrices, multiplying matrices, and calculating the inverse matrix, making them a powerful tool in linear algebra.

3.3.7. Handle complex data: It can be used to represent more complex data such as tables, mathematical matrices, images, graphs, and maps, making it useful in a variety of applications.

3.3.8. Ease of iteration: Iteration across two-dimensional arrays is simple and structured using nested loops, which facilitates the execution of repeated operations on the data.

3.3.9. Dynamic (in some languages): In some programming languages such as Python, two-dimensional arrays can be easily resized by adding or removing rows and columns, unlike other languages that require pre-allocation of memory.

Example of two-dimensional array applications:

- Graphics and images: Two-dimensional arrays can be used to represent images, where each element represents a pixel color.
- Electronic tables: Spreadsheets such as those in Excel programs can be represented using two-dimensional arrays.
- Scientific and engineering applications: used in linear algebra and matrix operations such as solving mathematical equations.
- Games: Used to store and update map and network data in video games.
  These characteristics make two-dimensional arrays a powerful and flexible tool for structured data processing in many areas. And two-dimensional arrays come with a range of features and disadvantages that must be considered when using them in programming.

3.4. Features of two-dimensional array.

3.4.1. Good organization of data: It allows organizing data into rows and columns, which facilitates understanding and handling of data.

3.4.2. Quick random access: Any element in the array can be accessed quickly using two indicators (to navigate through rows and columns).

3.4.3. Storage efficiency: Data is stored in successive locations of memory, making read and write operations more efficient compared to some other data structures.

3.4.4. Simplicity of iteration: Nested loops are easy to use for iterating across matrix elements and performing operations on them.

3.4.5. Support for mathematical operations: It allows many mathematical operations to be easily performed, such as adding and multiplying matrices.

3.4.6. Versatility: Can be used in a variety of applications such as graphics, spreadsheets, and table representation in databases.

3.5. Disadvantages of two-dimensional Arrays.

3.5.1. Fixed size: In most programming languages, the size of the array must be determined when it is created and cannot be changed later, which means that enough size must be allocated in advance.

3.5.2. Memory consumption: It can consume a large amount of memory, especially when dealing with large arrays, and this may be inefficient in terms of memory usage.

3.5.3. Difficulty adding and deleting: Adding or deleting rows or columns from an array can be a complex and expensive process in terms of time and memory, especially in languages that do not support dynamic structures.

3.5.4. Single-type limitations: Arrays only store elements of the same type, which can be inflexible in some applications that require storing different data types.

3.5.5. Inflexibility: Arrays are less flexible compared to some other data structures such as linked lists or sequential lists, which can easily change size.

3.5.6. Complex operations: Some operations on large arrays, such as sorting and searching, may be less efficient compared to some other data structures designed specifically for those operations.

3.6. When are two-dimensional Arrays used?

Optimal use Despite some drawbacks, two-dimensional arrays remain a powerful and effective tool when used in the right scenarios. They are ideal for use in applications that require organizing data in the form of fixed-sized tables where operations on elements are specific and straightforward.
They are used in a wide range of applications, especially when it is necessary to organize data in the form of a table or grid. Here are some common scenarios where two-dimensional arrays are used:

3.6.1. Table representation of data: When you need to represent data in the form of tables, such as:
- Spreadsheets: where data is organized into rows and columns.
- Timetables: for scheduling events or appointments.
- Database tables: to represent tables in databases.

3.6.2. Mathematical operations: Two-dimensional arrays are useful in various mathematical operations, such as:
- Mathematical array: To solve algebraic equations, arithmetic operations on array (e.g. addition and multiplication).
- Linear algebra: in applications involving arrays and vectors.

3.6.3. Drawings and images: Two-dimensional arrays are used to represent drawings and images:
- Digital images: where each element in the array represents a pixel in the image.
- Two-dimensional games: to represent maps and grids in games.

3.6.4. Data Analysis: In data science and data analysis, arrays are used to organize and store data for analysis:
- Statistical data: to store statistical data in a structured form.
- Big Data Analysis: To process large amounts of structured data.

3.6.5. Word processing: Two-dimensional arrays are used in applications that require word processing:
- Frequency tables: to analyze the frequency of words in texts.
- Search engines: to represent documentary arrays in search engines.

3.6.6. Networking applications: In some networking applications, two-dimensional arrays can be used:
- Graph representation: to represent the relationships between nodes (such as road network representation or social networks).
- Routing algorithms: to represent paths and cost between different points in the network.

3.6.7. Artificial Intelligence and Machine Learning: Two-dimensional matrices are used in AI and machine learning applications:
- Neora networks: to represent input data, weights and standards.
- Data analysis: To organize data into mathematical models used in machine learning.

3.6.8. Simulation and Modeling: In Simulation and Scientific Modeling:
- Modeling of physical systems: to represent physical models and simulation calculations.

- Numerical analysis: to solve differential equations and complex systems.
- **Conclusion**: Two-dimensional arrays are a powerful and flexible tool used in a wide range of applications where data requires structured structuring into rows and columns. The optimal choice for using two-dimensional arrays depends on the nature of the data and the operations that will be performed on these data.

This is a simple Python programming example of a student grade array that shows how to create and use two-dimensional arrays:

Suppose we have a class of students and each student has grades in three subjects. We will create a two-dimensional array to represent students' grades, and then calculate the average for each student and the average score for each subject.

```python
# Create the array
# Array representing the grades of 3 students in 3 subjects

grades = [
    [85, 90, 78], # First Student Grades
    [88, 92, 80], # Second Student Grades
    [90, 85, 85] # Third Student Grades
]

# Matrix printing

    print("Student Grades:")
    for row in grades:
        print(row)

# Calculate average grades for each student
```

```python
print("n/Average score per student:")
for i, row in enumerate(grades):
    average = sum(row) / len(row)
    print(f"student {i + 1}: {average:.2f}")
```

Calculate the average score for each subject

```python
num_students = len(grades)
num_subjects = len(grades[0])

print("n\Average score per subject:")
for j in range(num_subjects):
    subject_total = sum(grades[i][j] for i in range(num_students))
    subject_average = subject_total / num_students
    print(f"subject {j + 1}: {subject_average:.2f}")
```

Full Program
array representing the grades of 3 students in 3 subjects

```python
grades = [
    [85, 90, 78], # First Student Grades
    [88, 92, 80], # Second Student Grades
    [90, 85, 85] # Third Student Grades
]
```

Matrix printing

```python
Print("Student Grades:")
For row in grades:
    Print(row)
```

Calculate average grades for each student

```python
print("n\Average score per student:")
for i, row in enumerate(grades):
    average = sum(row) / len(row)
```

```python
    print(f"student {i + 1}: {average:.2f}")
# Calculate the average score for each subject

num_students = len(grades)
num_subjects = len(grades[0])

print("n\Average score per subject:")
for j in range(num_subjects):
    subject_total = sum(grades[i][j] for i in range(num_students))
    subject_average = subject_total / num_students
    print(f"subject {j + 1}: {subject_average:.2f}")
```

Code Explanation.

- Array creation: 'grades' is a 2D array that contains the grades of 3 students in 3 subjects.
- Array printing: The 'for' loop is used to print rows in the array.
- Calculate average scores for each student: Using 'enumerate', each class (each student's scores) is repeated and grades are averaged.
- Calculate the grade average for each subject: Using two overlapping loops, the grades for each subject are collected across all students and then the average is calculated.

This example shows how two-dimensional arrays can be used to store structured data in the form of a table and how to perform simple operations on them such as calculating averages.

❏ Static Data Structures
4. Tables.

4.1. What are Tables?

Tables in data structures are organizational structures used to store data in an orderly and orderly manner, and are an essential part of databases. Tables consist of rows and columns, where each row represents a single record and each column represents a type of field.

4.2. Components of tables:

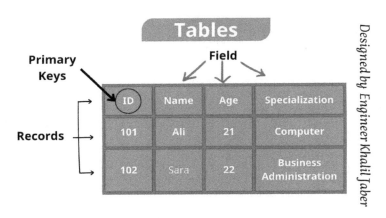

Designed by Engineer Khalil Jaber

Figure (53) illustrates table structures

4.2.1. Columns:
- Each column in the table represents a specific type of data.
- Columns contain a specific name and data type (such as integer, text, date, etc.).
- Columns can be compulsory (cannot be empty) or optional (can be empty).

4.2.2. Rows:
- Each row represents a single data record in the table.
- A row contains a set of values, each value for a specific column.
- Rows are commonly known as primary keys, which are unique to each row.

4.3.   Examples of using tables:

4.3.1. Student database.

- Table: Students.
- Columns: University ID, Name, Age, Specialization
- Grades: A record for each student that includes university number, name, age, Specialization

ID	Name	Age	Specialization
1001	Ali	21	Computer
1002	Sara	22	Business Adm.

Figure (54) Tables for the student database.

4.3.2. Sales Database:

- Table: Sales
- Columns: Invoice number, product name, quantity, price
- Rows: A record for each sale including invoice number, product name, quantity, price

Invoice number	product name	quantity	Price
401	A	100	3.5
402	B	53	2.0

Figure (55) Sales Database

4.4. Table types:

4.4.1. Simple tables: contain simple columns and rows and are used to store uncomplicated data.

4.4.2. Composite tables: Contain relationships between different tables, such as tables linked by foreign keys.

4.4.3. Tables provide an effective way to organize, access, and retrieve data, making them an essential element in database design and big data management.

4.5. What are the characteristics of tables?

Tables in data structures and databases have a set of characteristics that make them a powerful tool for organizing and managing data. Here are the most prominent features:

4.5.1. Structure of columns and rows:

- Columns: Represents data types, and each column has a unique name and a specific data type (such as text, number, date).
- Rows: Represents records, and each row contains specific data that corresponds to the columns.

4.5.2. Keys:
- Primary Key: A column or group of columns that ensures that each row in the table is unique. The primary key cannot contain duplicate or null values.
- Foreign Key: A column or set of columns that is used to create a relationship between two tables. The foreign key is linked to the primary key in another table.

4.5.3. Integrity and Restrictions:

- Data integrity: Rules that ensure the validity and accuracy of data, such as reference integrity that ensures that every value in the foreign key is in the primary key of the linked table.
- Constraints: Specifies additional rules on data, such as unique values, do not allow null values, or default values.

4.5.4. Queries: Data can be retrieved from tables using query languages such as SQL, allowing complex searches, filtering and sorting data.

4.5.5. Relationships: Tables can have relationships with other tables, enhancing the interdependence and integration of data. Types of relationships include:

      – One-to-One.

      – One-to-Many.

      – Many-to-Many.

4.5.6. Redundancy: Avoiding data duplication is a basic principle in table design, where relationships between tables can be used to store data in a non-duplicate form.

4.5.7. Sustainability: Tables can handle large amounts of data effectively, making them suitable for use in large and complex applications.

4.5.8. Indexing: Indexes are used to improve data retrieval speed. Indexes are usually based on the columns most commonly used in searches.

4.5.9. Security: Security measures can be applied to control access to data, such as read and write permissions at the table or column level.

These features make tables a powerful and flexible tool for storing and organizing data, making it easier to access and manage it efficiently and effectively.

4.6. When are tables used?

Tables are used in a variety of scenarios and applications, especially in the areas of data management and organization. Here are some common situations where tables are used:

4.6.1. Relational Databases:

- Tables are used to store and organize data in relational databases such as MySQL, PostgreSQL, Oracle Database, and Microsoft SQL Server.
- Used in applications that require complex data storage and advanced query operations.

4.6.2. Content Management Systems (CMS): In websites that use content management systems such as WordPress or Drupal, tables are used to store user information, articles, comments, and settings.

4.6.3. Commercial Applications:
- Companies use tables to store customer data, products, orders, and invoices.
- Used in customer relationship management (CRM) and ERP applications.

4.6.4. Financial applications: Tables are used in banks and financial institutions to store data on accounts, transactions, loans, and investments.

4.6.5. Human Resource Management: Used to store employee data, payroll records, performance appraisals, and manage attendance and leave.

4.6.6. Health systems: Hospitals and clinics use schedules to store patient data, medical records, appointments, and medical bills.

4.6.7. Education: Educational institutions use schedules to store student data, grades, schedules, and courses.

4.6.8. Scientific research: Tables are used to store experimental data, research results, and surveys.

4.6.9. E-commerce: Used in e-commerce sites to store product data, users, orders, and comments.

4.6.10. Project Management: Schedules are used to store data on projects, tasks, participating members, and timelines.

4.6.11. Government Applications: Government agencies use tables to store citizen data, statistics, official records, and services provided.

4.6.12. Personal applications: Schedules can be used in personal applications such as managing to-do lists, tracking budget, organizing work schedules and studying.

4.7. Benefits of using tables:

- Organization: Tables allow data to be organized logically and easily understand.
- Efficiency: Tables enable data retrieval quickly and effectively.
- Relationships: allows the establishment of relationships between different types of data, which promotes integration and interdependence.
- Scalability: Tables can handle large amounts of data while maintaining good performance.

In short, tables are used everywhere data needs to be stored in an orderly manner that can be easily retrieved and analyzed.

4.8. What is the difference between matrices and tables?

Arrays and tables are data structures used to store data, but there are fundamental differences between them in how data is organized and used. Here's the difference between them:

- **Arrays**:

 - Structure: An array is a collection of similar elements stored in a contiguous location in memory. Elements can be integers, decimals, or Pointers.
 - Access: Any element in the array can be accessed directly using the index. The latency of any element is constant ($O(1)$).
 - Dimension: Matrices can be one-dimensional (1D) or multidimensional (2D, 3D, ...).
 - Size: The size of the array is fixed after it is created, and can only be changed by creating a new array and moving the elements to it.
 - Performance: Arrays are faster to perform when accessing or modifying elements, because they use memory continuously.

- **Tables**.

 - Structure: A table is a collection of data stored in the form of rows and columns. Data in columns can be of different types (such as integers, text, logical values, etc.).
 - Access: Data in the table can be accessed by row column names and indexes. Accessing data can be more complex compared to arrays.
 - Dimension: Tables are mainly two-dimensional (rows x columns).
 - Size: The table can be resized by adding or deleting rows and columns as you need.

- Performance: Tables may be slower in performance when accessing or modifying data, especially if they contain a large amount of data and are complex in their structure.

Examples of use:

- Arrays: Widely used in applications that require intensive calculations such as image processing, games, and physical simulations.
- Tables: Commonly used in databases where you need to store and retrieve structured data such as records and attributes in data management applications.

In short, arrays are simpler and faster to handle similar, fixed-sized data, while tables are more flexible and used to store diverse and variable data.

▪ **A code example that illustrates tables:**

Using the 'pandas' library in Python can manipulate tables (DataFrames). Here's a simple example of how to create a table and perform some basic operations on it:

```
import pandas as pd
```

Create a spreadsheet (DataFrame)

```
import pandas as pd
data = {
    'Name': ['Ahmed', 'Mona', 'Ali', 'Sara'],
    'Age': [23, 45, 34, 22],
    'City': ['Cairo', 'Alexandria', 'Giza', 'Port Said']
}
df = pd.DataFrame(data)
```

Print Table

```python
    print("Original table:")
    print(df)
```

Add a new column

```python
df['Salary'] = [5000, 7000, 6000, 5500]
```

Print table after adding column

```python
print("n\Table after adding salary column:")
print(df)
```

Filter rows by specific condition

```python
df_filtered = df[df['age'] < 30]
```

Print table after filtering

```python
print("n\Table after filtering ages greater than 30:")
print(df_filtered)
```

Calculate Age Average

```python
average_age = df['age'].mean()
print(f"n\Median age: {average_age}")
```

- **Code Explanation:**

- Import the Pandas library: We import the 'pandas' library that is used to handle tables in Python.
- Create spreadsheet: We create a dictionary containing data (names, ages, cities), and then we create a DataFrame from this dictionary.

- Print the original table: We print the original table to see the data.
- Add New Column: We add a new Salaries column to the table.
- Print the table after adding the column: We print the table after adding the salary column.
- Filter rows: We filter rows where they are older than 30.
- Print table after filtering: We print table after filtering.
- Calculate life expectancy: We calculate the average age and print the result.

Using the 'pandas' library makes working with attributes in Python easy and efficient.

End of Chapter 4

End of Part One

For more information about data structures, read the book Data Structures Part II.

You can also follow the author's videos in Arabic on Jaber's YouTube channel.

www.youtube.com/@jaberinfo

I am waiting for your comments on my following
email:Khaliljaber99@gmail.com

Or on WhatsApp

00962795978795

Many thanks

www.ingramcontent.com/pod-product-compliance
Lightning Source LLC
LaVergne TN
LVHW081522050326
832903LV00025B/1592